Otherwise, I'm Fine

OTHERWISE, I'M FINE

a memoir

BARBARA PRESNELL

THE UNIVERSITY OF
SOUTH CAROLINA PRESS

© 2025 Barbara Presnell

Published by the University of South Carolina Press
Columbia, South Carolina 29208

uscpress.com

Printed in the United States of America

Library of Congress Cataloging-in-Publication Data
can be found at https://lccn.loc.gov/2024049304

ISBN: 978-1-64336-506-0 (hardcover)
ISBN: 978-1-64336-561-9 (ebook)

For Mama and Daddy.
From us.

Come back. Even as a shadow, even as a dream.
—Euripedes, "Herakles"

What is grief, if not love persevering?
—Vision, *WandaVision*

Prologue

My father didn't have to die twice, but he did, first from a failed surgery and second from my mother's words: "We won't talk about him. It'll be easier that way."

No one mentioned him except a friend, new to town, who wanted details I refused to provide and, almost ten years later when I was in my early twenties, an older woman who asked how I was doing with his death.

"I hate him," I told her, without hesitation. "If he'd loved me, he would have lived." She was surprised by my response, questioned it, but never asked again. Hate was the easiest way to excise him from my memory. Denial was a close second.

But when loss piles on to loss, as happened to me, its weight increasing like snow on a roof, eventually the rafters give way, and the house comes down.

My house had begun its collapse, but I didn't know it yet, that muggy July morning in 1985, sixteen years after his death, when I drove an hour and a half from my Somerset, Kentucky, home to Lexington. I found the clinic office tucked in a shopping center less than a mile from the sprawling campus of the University of Kentucky.

A few months earlier, I'd left my college teaching job in North Carolina to join my husband, Bill, in southeastern Kentucky where he'd taken a job as a reporter for the statewide newspaper. In addition to being unemployed and in a state where I knew no one, I was four months into my third pregnancy with no child born, and I was scared to death.

Helen, my new therapist sat across from me in a green uphol-stered chair, her hands cupping the ends of its arms, her wrists heavy with bracelets. I'd sunk into the deep sofa opposite her, my legs crossed, my arms folded above the pooch of my growing belly.

I liked her immediately, her smile, the way she focused in on me, as though I mattered. She didn't take notes. Instead, she leaned in and listened, smiling, in a way that told me whatever I said would be all right. I'd spent most of my life learning how to lie. Telling the truth didn't come naturally for me, but something about her made me feel safe enough to try honesty for a change.

My obstetrician had assured me all was well with the pregnancy, but I didn't believe him. My sadness following two miscarriages within the last year was so severe that some nights my whole body ached as I lay in bed trying to sleep. I knew how to lose things, I reminded myself. Don't get too confident, don't hope too much. A healthy, growing fetus at four months should have been reason to feel hopeful. Any minute, I expected blood to spill again, and this latest life to end.

"What is wrong with you?" Bill had asked over and over. "Why can't you be happy?"

I didn't know. Happy was not something I was. Every gurgle in my stomach, every heartburn in my chest or pain in my belly felt like another death was imminent. That was why I was here, I told Helen as we began.

She asked about my family. Brother, yes, and sister, both older. No, I don't see them often. We've never been close. Mother? Still living, I told her. Educated, hardworking, a bit overprotective.

"Your father? Tell me about him."

I hesitated, as I always did. My chest squeezed, and I looked away. "He died." I couldn't keep my voice from shaking. My eyes pooled with tears, and I couldn't stop that either, though I did my best to blink them away.

At night, lying in bed not sleeping, I would pull the twin frame of my parents' photos from the top of my nightstand and stare into my father's face, remembering him, listening for his voice, and if I could only hear it, imagine what he'd say to me. I was supposed to have forgotten about him years ago; instead, I carried him around with me daily, unable to let him go.

She nudged forward. I'd caught her attention. "I'm very sorry. Recently?"

"Um, sixteen years."

"Sixteen years? What happened?"

Behind her, books on psychology, literature, and art lined her shelves. She handed me a box of tissue, a dead giveaway that I wasn't fooling her.

"It's not something I talk about," I finally said.

I hadn't forgotten the smell of his soap or his big ears. I hadn't forgotten the kitten fluff of his hair on those nights he would let me rub his head as he sat reading in the recliner. I hadn't forgotten his voice on those afternoons when he pushed open the back door, home from the textile mill, and called out, "Law me!" to anyone near enough to hear him. Or how he'd unknot his tie and wrestle the top button of his shirt free, and soon he'd head out the back door in his Bermuda shorts and loafers, hauling dirt into Mama's new azalea garden, dragging rocks to the back yard, his suit and tie tossed into a chair in the bedroom.

Helen scooted so close to the edge of her chair I thought she was going to stand. "Sixteen years, and you don't talk about it?" No one had ever spoken to me that way before, so direct and intense, and it was oddly comforting.

"Do you see you are living on a fault line?"

I was startled. His heart had always been my heart, his brown hair my brown hair, that way he stood with his hands behind his back the way I stood with my hands behind my back, but I knew better than to talk about him.

Her words rang through my head, crisp and lingering: You are living on a fault line.

I knew she was right the minute she said it. She'd found me out, uncovered my secret. My father had died. I had missed him every single day for sixteen years. I was holed up in a broken house of old grief, deep sorrow, a daughter's inability to let go, and the walls around me were beginning to crumble.

CHAPTER 1

In the only photograph that exists of my father and me, I'm three years old and nestled between his knees on the front porch step of the High Street house, a small one-story we'd soon grow out of. It's Easter Sunday. My bell-shaped coat is buttoned up to its collar, my head covered in a wool bonnet that cups my ears and ties beneath my chin. My basket, shreds of Easter grass spilling over the edges, is tilted in my lap. I'm looking down, digging through the basket, perhaps to curl my fingers around a dyed egg or maybe to discover a loose jellybean. His arms wrap around my elbows. Other black-and-white photos from those years are stuffed into brown envelopes and stored in the musty secretary in my living room, but this is the only one that includes just the two of us. Edwin, older by five years, and Ellen in the exact middle at two and a half years, always appeared with me in other photos—in the plastic swimming pool, on the porch steps in Sunday outfits, in our snow-covered yard bundled in coats and boots. I wanted my father to be mine, only mine, to love me best, but in pictures, we are equally his.

He did love me, though I no longer believe—or need to—that he loved me best. We were alike, he and I. I loved what he loved— fishing, working in the yard, planting azaleas, fixing things that broke, building things, inventing things. We'd climb down the back porch steps together to the basement, and he'd tinker, tossing aside scraps of wood I could carve into animals or hammer together into bird houses while he worked on his own projects like tables or bookshelves. I'd follow him through the mill on Saturdays when he'd go in to check on a machine or grab a package of newly sewn T-shirts. I wanted to be where he was, loved when somebody on the line, a sewer or a knitter, would say, "Is that your little girl, Bill?" He'd cup his hand around my shoulder and say, "This one's my baby," smiling.

I loved the way his whole body would become twenty-five years younger when he started telling war stories, no matter who was listening. After supper, he'd pull out photographs and scrapbooks and reminisce while he kept an eye on *Gunsmoke* or *The Man from U.N.C.L.E.* In summers, he'd gather in the front yard with his buddies—some men he'd grown up with, some old veterans from his company—and they'd tell war stories until Mama called him in because it was getting late, and she knew he'd stay out all night if somebody was there to swap stories with. He'd bring coworkers home from the mill, and they'd follow him through the kitchen into the den, where Ellen and I would be listening to music and doing homework, and he'd pull his copy of *The Last Battle* off the shelf and open it to the page that told his story. They'd slap his back and tell him how great it was, "and to think Cornelius Ryan himself sat in your living room!" He also stood straighter those afternoons, his grin a little wider, and, later, he'd beam all through supper with the family. The war made him more than the country boy who joined up, more than the shipping clerk from the mill who went off to training camp. I watched that transformation as his past became his present, but I did not understand it.

I was his shadow, his partner, his assistant, co-conspirator, his third child, the baby. Where he went, I went. What he did, I did too. This was how I knew his love and, surely, how he knew mine.

∞

My third-grade teacher, Mrs. Moffitt, had been designing projects so her students could explore the world of science. Science was not my strong subject, but if it involved making things—and in this case it did—I was enthusiastic. Already Daddy and I had built a motor that ran off a nine-volt battery, generated static electricity that could make my hair stand straight up, and poured soda and vinegar in a bottle so the chemical reaction blew up a balloon by itself.

One spring night, I lingered at the kitchen table after supper, turning the pages of my science book, while Daddy finished washing dishes. My homework assignment, due the next day, was to come up with an experiment I could share with the class, and I was stuck.

Edwin and Ellen had left the dinner table for the den to finish their homework. After clearing the table, Mama, who was teaching eighth-grade social studies by then, excused herself to grade a stack of tests before bedtime.

Finished, Daddy tossed the wet dish towel onto the countertop, turned to me, and said,

"All right, I've got an idea for you. I learned this trick when I was your age. You'll be amazed." He smiled, drawing on a half-smoked cigarette. "Go get a glass and fill it half full of water and bring me a saucer from the cabinet."

He'd taken off his tie and rolled up the sleeves of his white work shirt. The eczema that covered his hands and wrists was red after being in dishwater. He'd soak them later in cream and wear gloves to bed. If the eczema bothered him, and it must have, he didn't say. I had eczema too, another connection I thought made me his special child.

I pushed a stool over so I could reach the middle shelf by the sink, grabbed a lime green plate, and pulled down a jelly glass, which I half filled with tap water, and brought them to the table.

"You're gonna love this." He blew out a last puff of smoke and stubbed the butt of his cigarette in the ashtray on the table. In his other hand was a candle I hadn't seen him get from the junk drawer, the kind we melted down onto plates when the power went out and put in our brass candlesticks when company came for dinner.

I squeezed next to him and watched as he fixed the candle on the plate and poured the water onto the saucer the way he did with his morning coffee to cool it in a hurry. Then he reached into his shirt pocket for a pack of matches, lit the candle, and placed the glass over it. In seconds, the water swept up into the glass, extinguishing the candle, whose wick perched just above the water line.

I laughed. "Do it again!" It was magic, every bit as good as the nine-volt battery engine and the balloon blowing itself full of air. He lifted the glass, breaking the tight seal around it, and water spilled back into the saucer. Again, he lit the candle, placed the glass over it, and the glass sucked up the water as the candle went out.

He was laughing now too, as pleased as I was. "The empty glass creates a vacuum. The heat from the candle soaks up all the oxygen which makes the candle die out, and it pulls up all the water. The candle's out but the glass is full. How about that?"

I was a long way from understanding the science behind his trick. What I knew of vacuums came from Mama's Electrolux, which sucked up dirt as easily as this glass sucked up water. A tight seal prevented the water from spilling out until Daddy pried it loose.

He smiled, leaned back in his chair, pulled another cigarette from his pack of Winstons and lit it, then pushed the matchbook toward me. This is how he loved me. We sat in the kitchen, darkness creeping in the windows, and while he watched, I lit the candle again and again, closed the glass over it, and as water rose and snuffed the light, our joy and our laughter mingled together, as though we had all the time and all the light in the world.

In the spring of my fifth-grade year, we moved up the hill to a new house on Ridgecrest Road, a patch of woods the only barrier between the old house and the new. Mama saw a photograph of her dream house in a magazine, and Daddy ordered blueprints. It was spacious, a modern ranch house in a desirable neighborhood with opportunity for a beautiful yard.

At the end of the street and around the corner was the Pritchard house where twenty of us neighborhood girls gathered weekly for Girl Scout meetings led by Mrs. Pritchard, a strong-willed mother determined to turn us into young ladies whether we wanted it or not. In early autumn of our seventh-grade year, to earn our Social Dancing merit badge in her attempt to fill our sashes front and back, she invited the twenty-some young men of the Boy Scout troop across town to join us for a dance. That Saturday night, as music wafted from a stereo and lights in her basement flickered low, I found a corner by the door, wished I were invisible, waited in sheer agony as time crept by. The more confident seventh graders eased onto the dance floor, either bobbing up and down to the music, looking in any direction except at each other, or clinging together so tightly that little air flowed between them.

I watched my friend Nancy and her boyfriend, Jimmy, who was two grades ahead of us, how he pulled her right up against his chest, his head on her shoulder, his eyes closed, his arms squeezing around her. It was a wonder she could breathe. She looked up, saw me staring, and smiled in that way she had that let me know she had a boyfriend, and I did not.

Earlier in the night, I kept an eye on Al, who I sort of liked but who hadn't looked at me, not even to say hey, let alone ask me to dance. I thought how different this might all be if my would-be boyfriend Ricky were here with me, and then I'd show Nancy. I'd known Ricky, one year older, all my life because he lived next door to us on High Street. I played baseball with him for all those years, caught crawdads in the creek that ran between our houses, and let him kiss me once in the Haithcock's chicken coop. That seemed to me to be the makings of the perfect boyfriend.

At school earlier that week I had walked over to the eighth-grade hallway—even though I was the only seventh grader there—so I could find him when he came out of class. He smiled when he saw me, and I said, "Would you like to go with me to the Girl Scout dance on Saturday night?"

"I can't," he said. "I've got a girlfriend." Which I didn't know but should have.

That moment confirmed the truth: I was ugly, pimples starting to pop up on my forehead, my hair so poufy that I wore a ball cap to breakfast every morning to tame it, even though the result was an indentation—ball-cap head—around my hair all day at school. And on top of that, I never wore the right clothes, I never spoke up in class, and I was not popular like Ricky was. Plus, I suspected Ricky was smoking cigarettes, and I wasn't. Yet.

I wasn't watching Bruce, because I knew he didn't like me, but that night, Bruce did what I wanted to do: he climbed out of Mrs. Pritchard's basement window and ran as far away from that dance as he could, half the boys cheering him on. He made it as far as Lindley Park School before Mr. Pritchard caught him, brought him back, and called his parents.

At ten o'clock on the dot, Mrs. Pritchard turned on the bright overhead light, blew her whistle, and said, "Party's over!"

Daddy had pulled Mama's Chevrolet station wagon, its engine idling, up to the curb in line with the rest of the parents picking up their sons and daughters. October air was warm enough that he had rolled the driver's side window down. His arm was hanging out, a cigarette dangling between his fingers, its smoke curling up into the night like a genie's wisp of cloud.

I had tears in my eyes before I reached the car, but nobody could see them because it was dark. I got in, pulled the door to, slumped down in my seat. "Let's go."

"That bad?" Daddy took a puff then tossed the butt out on the road and rolled up the window. I didn't say anything, and I tried not to let him see my face. I didn't look out the window to watch my friends climbing in their parents' cars, some with their boyfriends.

"Wanna ride around some?" He was looking at me, jingling the car key. "Want to go by the drive-in and get a sundae before we go home?" He knew what I needed more than I did. He knew how to love a woman, even if that woman was his twelve-year-old daughter. Especially her.

But I shook my head. I didn't know then how much I needed what he had to offer. What I thought I wanted to do was crawl into my pajamas, turn out the light, and listen to radio talk shows, imagining I lived somewhere in Texas or worked as a waitress in Phoenix.

He cranked the engine, and we pulled out and onto the street.

"Scoot over here," he said when we got to the first stop sign. He patted the seat beside him. The ashtray was open in front, the dashboard glowing a soft green and white. I scooted across the long seat next to him, snuggling in like I did when I was seven and he let me drive. Little girl, young woman, it didn't matter. He draped his right arm over my shoulder, steered with his left.

We rode like that, cruising down Sunset Avenue, circling neighborhoods on the other side of town, taking the long way home, until we turned onto our street and pulled into our driveway. He eased the Chevrolet into the carport, cut off the engine, and squeezed my shoulder as I slid back over to my side and reached for the door handle. The house was dark except for one yellow light in the den where Mama was reading the afternoon paper, waiting on us—the daughter she never could understand, and the man who loved her almost as much as he loved me.

I'd seen the signs—we all had—that something was wrong. The way we'd find him home asleep in the afternoons when he should have been at work. His loss of appetite, his inability to eat much, even when he was hungry. His refusal to see a doctor. If he complained, he was never where we children could hear him. He said he was fine. Everybody knew he wasn't, but nobody said it.

One night toward dawn, I was startled awake by noises familiar and frightening. Inside my room the heavy green curtains were drawn, and no light crept in at the edges. I could see the numbers on my clock radio that read 5:30 in white numbers. An hour and a half before I had to get up for school. I pulled the cover to my neck, turned to my right side, and tried to sleep.

Again, I heard them, coming from behind the wall on the other side of my bed, from the green bathroom, the one I shared with Edwin, Ellen, and Daddy, so Mama could use the pink one for her bathing and dressing. I heard coughing. Then deep-throated gagging. Then splashing into the toilet as though someone had turned a hose into it. A flush. This time, I allowed myself to know what it was.

My eyes were open now, my body tense. The bathroom went quiet, and I heard soft footsteps in the hallway, a tap-tap on the bathroom door, and my mother's voice as she called my father's name, "Bill. Bill, are you all right?"

His answer was muffled by the wall and the closed door.

"Is there anything I can do?"

The creak of the door handle, the door swishing open over the carpet.

"Come on to bed then. Drink some Maalox. It'll settle your stomach."

My parents' bedroom door closed. I could hear their voices resonating against the walls and gently bouncing off the chest of drawers, the pink chair, Mama's black pocketbook dropped onto the cushion and open slightly, but I couldn't hear their words. Light crept from under their door, stayed on a minute. Went off.

I couldn't go back to sleep. Pretty soon, I climbed out from under the covers, tucked my pillow under my arm, and walked across the hall to my sister Ellen's room, where, without making a sound, I slipped between the sheets of her extra twin bed and lay there, shivering, until it was daylight, and I felt my sister shaking my shoulder.

"What are you doing in here? You need to get up. Daddy's got breakfast on the table. It's a school day." Ellen, my protector, my comforter, in those early days.

"It was Daddy, in the bathroom. It woke me up."

She didn't say anything, but looked toward the window where the blue curtains had been pulled back, and morning sun streaked in. "All right," she said. "All right."

If he really loved me, I thought, he'd find a way to live. He wouldn't open the car door and vomit in the road when he was taking me to school. He wouldn't lie on the couch in the middle of the afternoon when my friends were over. But what was eating up his stomach was stronger than family, than work, friends, or children. It was stronger than mortar fire, strong enough to take him down when the daily pounding of war had not. He really did love me, of that I'm certain, but he could not keep the light of his own candle from snuffing out, even for me.

CHAPTER 2

My husband, Bill, and I pedal down Railroad Grade Road alongside the South Fork, past freshly built log cabins, old farmhouses, dense woods, and lush fields on which cows graze. We've rented bikes from the River Girl Fishing Company, close to the Todd General Store in North Carolina, two hours from home. Autumn in the mountains means multicolored leaves clinging to trees and drifting all around us on the road. The air is crisp and warm, and we have peeled off our jackets and stuffed them in our packs.

I'm riding behind Bill along the flat road beside the New River, watching the awkwardness of his muscled legs on the bike. A two-speed rider from childhood, he's never mastered multiple gears and prefers to stay in fifth or sixth, his legs and arms doing the work of climbing hills or slowing his speed. Often, he stands, pumping his legs hard into the pedals, the way a boy of the sixties would race through neighborhoods, playing cards flap-flapping in the spokes of his wheels.

Beyond the second bridge on Railroad Grade Road, we pull our bikes into the grass, prop them against a tree, and climb down to the river so we can kick off our shoes and dangle our feet in the water while we munch on turkey sandwiches and apples and share a bottle of chardonnay.

"I've got an idea," I say. "Let's walk that map. Let's just do it."

He knows what I mean, my father's road map through France in 1944, yellow and fragile, folded to pocket-size, with a distinct red ink line that zigzags from small town to small town headed east toward Belgium. I found it among his World War II army memorabilia. My father, William G. "Bill" Presnell was a first sergeant in the 30th Infantry Division, and an important part of his job was keeping records, many of which were never collected by the army after the war. His small archive includes letters and maps; a stuffed scrapbook, its leather binding worn apart; a ledger with a roster of his company and records of those killed in action, missing in action, or suffering battle fatigue and other ailments; and an album with more than three thousand photographs, some labeled, most of them not.

"Save these papers and the other stuff," my father had written in a letter back home to his sister, Alma, dated early 1945, that I had found tucked in a corner of his trunk. "I'll get them from you when I get home." I pictured large boxes of items arriving on her Laurinburg, North Carolina, doorstep, her sifting through her youngest brother's collection.

The scrapbook he eventually put together chronicles his company's journey from Glasgow, Scotland, to Magdeburg, Germany. His sources were news clippings from the hometown paper as well as *Stars and Stripes,* obits, postcards, and top secret memos from headquarters. His handwritten blue ledger records daily troop movements, battles during that same period, and occasional days of rest.

Stark black-and-white photos in the album capture a story of the day-to-day life of the average infantrymen. Soldiers, including my father, drape their arms around young women or roll cigarettes beside bombed-out buildings. Bridges, orchards, sheep in fields, chow lines, individuals and groups in various configurations—the wire section, intelligence, the radio division, and the cooking crew —appear in now faded images. An older man he identifies as "Father Sullivan" shows up more than once, and an entire page is dedicated to an amusing collection of the backs of young men standing in front of latrines, peering over their shoulders into the camera. Looking at the faces in the photographs, I can imagine what my father's life as a young soldier might have been, a complex mix of exhaustion, camaraderie, and laughter found in the most mundane moments.

My idea to walk the map hasn't come out of the blue. Since bringing his "army stuff," as we call it, home from my mother's house to store in my attic a few years back, I've been thinking. The papers are fragile, the scrapbook falling apart, and I've pored over it like an archaeologist with her brush, reading the detail, trying to rebuild his story.

"Are you with me?" I ask Bill. A career journalist, he loves investigative writing, and asking questions is his strength. "I could take a semester off from teaching. I'm sure you could get some time off from work. We can travel the same roads if they're still there. We can talk to people."

His smile is all I need to know he's on board.

"What about Edwin and Ellen?" he asks.

"They're not going." I tug my shoe over my socked foot and retie the strings, careful not to lose my balance on the bank.

"He's their father, too," he says. "Whether they want them or not, the boxes belong to them as much as they belong to you, don't they?"

Yes, it's true. When I hauled the stuff home a few years back, we agreed I was storing it, not claiming it as my own. But neither has expressed interest in them since.

"All right. I'll ask them if I can use it, but that's all. I don't think they will care." The idea adds an uncomfortable wrinkle to my plan, but I know Bill's right. I have to ask.

That night, home long enough to settle into the house, I sit at my computer and compose a single email to both siblings.

"Here's what Bill and I want to do," I begin. I detail our idea, perhaps too much, I realize later. I make it sound too good, too exciting, too important. I tell them of our plans to begin at Omaha Beach, to travel our father's exact route, maybe even find some people who appear in the photographs. "There's going to be wear and tear on the army stuff if we start digging around in it, so I need to know if it's okay with you both if we use it."

I hit send.

The next morning is a school day, and I wake early, so I can hit the road to campus ahead of my first class. On the way out the door, I check my email. Two answers wait in my inbox.

"If you're going, I'm going too," writes Ellen, who lives thirty minutes from me, though we see each other only a few times a year. Edwin, from his home in Georgia, replies, "You're not going without me."

All I can think is no. No.

I drive to the university and teach my classes, but my mind is not on crafting a good sentence or adding detail to a paragraph. All day, I'm inventing excuses in my head. How can I tell them no, that they aren't invited? How can I explain that I can't share this journey with them, don't want to, the distance between us too great? This trip is for me.

That night, I wait to hear the steady hum of Bill's CPAP machine that tells me he's fast asleep before I climb the stairs to the second floor where I keep an office. I open the attic door, drop to my knees, and drag out the storage box that holds my father's uniform. When we lived in the Ridgecrest Road house, the heavy wool jacket and pants hung in Ellen's extra closet, ready to be lifted off the hanger and draped onto someone's shoulders. Every summer, we'd pull it out and air it on the backyard clothesline before tucking it back into its spot in the closet, beside the artificial Christmas to-piaries and the spring hats. After Ellen and I left for college, Mama bought a wardrobe storage box, folded the uniform inside, sprinkled mothballs across the chest and sleeves, and packed it away in the attic. Every year, when the mothballs would disintegrate, she'd add more. When we cleaned out her house in Asheboro, North Carolina, after she died, we found empty seed pods left by squirrels or mice inside the box and small holes on the pocket and chest of the thin shirt, whether the result of chewing or dry rot, we weren't sure, Along with the other artifacts, I brought the box containing the uniform to my home and stored it in my attic, adding a fresh scatter of mothballs.

It's a standard issue uniform. On the top of the pile is an olive wool jacket with nickel-sized brass buttons down the front and on the cuffs and brass US insignia buttons on the collar. On one sleeve is the First Sergeant patch with three chevrons pointed down, two pointed up, and a diamond in the middle and on the other the 30th Infantry Division "Old Hickory" patch—three royal blue Roman numeral *X*s inside an *H* bordered with an *O* on a bright red background. Folded beneath the jacket is a khaki-colored cotton shirt, long-sleeved, its fabric so old that it is stiff beneath my touch, and so dry it crinkles when I rub it between my fingers. And beneath the shirt, olive wool pants with a button fly are folded with a crease that has fixed into a permanent line along the front legs.

I lift out the heavy jacket, made for cold-weather wear, then ease the fragile, almost waxy khaki shirt out of the box and unbutton the front, fearing each buttonhole will tear if I tug too hard. I slide my arms in and gently rebutton it to my neck. It's a snug fit, but it's a fit.

Next the jacket. First one arm and then the other into the sleeves, and one by one I fasten buttons up to the notch lapel.

Another near-perfect fit. I slip out of my jeans and step into the wool pants. Bill Presnell in 1945, according to his military records, weighed just shy of 135 pounds—my weight—and stood 5 feet 11 inches, three inches taller than me—a tall, skinny, country boy. I step my right leg in and then my left and begin to pull. The waist of the pants barely reaches my hips when it stops and won't go any higher. The cuffed ends drop down onto my feet, but I can't squeeze the waist past my hips. I could twist and pull, but in fear of tearing them, I slide the legs down and step out.

In the full-length mirror, I study the top half of myself. The jacket tugs neatly across my shoulders, the cuffs falling at the mid-point of my wrists. I look in my face and see in my square jaw an image of my father at war. I don't look like a soldier; I look like the aging daughter of that young man. Still, at that moment, something besides fabric wraps around me.

The sleeves around my arms belonged to a healthy man, young and strong, his future in front of him, dreaming about the children he might have one day. The sleeves belonged to a time back when the world was his, and he knew it, and he was somebody, somebody important, somebody a lot of soldiers depended on.

I sit in the soft chair by the window, letting my arms be his arms, my chest his chest. I grow warm in his woolen jacket, even though the upstairs rooms are chilly. A full hour later I unbutton the brass fasteners down the front jacket and tug the cuffs to slip the sleeves off my arms. Then the shirt. Instead of returning it to the box, I slide the jacket onto wooden hangers from the upstairs closet that used to be my son's. Shoulders take shape, wrists seem to reach out from empty cuffs.

I hear a voice, as clearly as if the speaker were sitting beside me. "This is not something I meant just for you," it says. "Take them along."

Only twice in my years without him has my father made his presence known: once, to bless his grandson, his namesake, shortly after the child's birth; later, to encourage my writing during a low period. I'm not given to hearing voices, so when one breaks in, I listen.

CHAPTER 3

It's mid-July in North Carolina with ninety-five-degree days soon to come, and I've turned the air conditioner on upstairs as though I'm expecting heat to rise. Ellen arrives first that Saturday morning and follows me up the steep, narrow stairs to my office. She holds tight to the rail, hesitating on each step to gauge the pain in her knees, which throb with arthritis.

"Send Edwin up when he gets here," I say to Bill. My sister has driven the thirty-five miles from Greensboro, North Carolina, for this planning meeting, and my brother left his home in Augusta, Georgia, as the sun was rising, hoping to arrive by midmorning. He'll make the three-hour trip back at the end of our meeting. His desire to drive six hours to help plan our trip surprises me and, at the same time, suggests that he might really want this sibling trip to happen. Ellen is sacrificing a day with her grandchildren, days she rarely foregoes. I don't yet trust their intentions, but I go along. Five of us have signed on for this journey: Ellen; her husband, David; Edwin; Bill; and me.

Two concerns have surfaced for me as we discuss this three-week trip together: first is my hesitation to dive headfirst into this difficult trek into my past with anyone, let alone my two siblings, the two who lived it with me; second is that of the five of us, only Bill and I have traveled Europe. We travel independently, planning our own lodging, food, travel, and leisure. We're comfortable if not confident in our ability to move freely, relying on others when we are lost or confused. This trip, as I envision it, must be carefully planned and executed if we are going to accomplish what I hope. Taking the others feels like responsibility I am not sure I'm ready for, not sure I want.

Ellen carries a bulging yellow plastic bag from an office supply store. "I thought we might need these." She spreads highlighter pens, paper clips, and Post-it notes in multiple colors across the coffee table. Earlier this morning, I brought an extra rocker to the upstairs room, so the three of us could circle around that table. She sits on the edge of the blue upholstered chair. I take the desk chair, its leather cushion wheezing when I sit.

I sense her nervousness, or else it's my own I'm attributing to her. As children, Edwin and Ellen were the best of friends. As young adults with growing families, they chatted on the phone regularly, and Ellen loved his two daughters almost as much as her own.

What happened between them I'll never know, but, these days, tension is more apparent than affection. He brags too much, drinks too much, parties too much, she says; she dotes on her grandchildren, sticks her nose in other people's business, especially his, he says. Their squabbles and complaints seem deeper than their petty grievances, and if I could understand the deep rift that divides them, I'd do what I could to close it. Instead, I am the sounding board, the go-between. I listen to both but don't intervene. "I'll give him a kidney if he ever needs it," Ellen said to me recently. "But he still makes me furious." I take the promise of a kidney as a sign of progress.

I hear the crunch of tires on gravel, the side door opening and closing, and then my brother's distinct voice, "God help me get up these stairs." He's tall, over six feet, and while he isn't overly heavy, he carries a lot of weight on small bones. One knee surgery behind him, he's expecting another in a few years. After cautious hugs, he eases onto the daybed across from Ellen and me. He's wearing a Clemson orange T-shirt over khaki shorts. He snaps the ball cap from his head and waves it as hello. "All right, Sister," he says to me. "What do we do now?"

For all my life, it seems, my siblings talked over me or for me, made decisions on my behalf, left me out of discussions, not taken me seriously. I'm serious now. I want to be in charge.

To establish my authority, a few days ago, I sent them an agenda of what we need to accomplish on this planning day—we will study maps and plan a route, choose dates for travel, allocate research assignments, and more. If we are going to do this and do it together, we have to work together, preferably with me as the boss.

"How long do you have today?" I ask both.

"I'm here as long as I need to be," Edwin says, unloading books from his briefcase and stacking them on the coffee table.

Ellen ruffles through a leather binder left over from her working days. "We're having leftovers for dinner, so I don't have to cook," she says. "I've got all day."

In addition to the agenda, I made up a list of "rules," which I distribute and give them a minute to review. My list imagines three groups of travelers, our routes intersecting at various points during our war route but separate at all other times. We'd all want it that way, I assumed when I wrote it. Too much time together could only be bad.

"Anything you want to add?" I ask. Both heads nod no.

They're so serious it's scary. I feel like I'm in a club meeting in a treehouse, and it's my club with my rules.

I pause and carry on. A couple of days ago, also planning for this meeting, I'd taken our father's 1944 map of France, the one he folded to a tight square and tucked away in his army trunk at the end of the war, to our local copy shop for color reproduction. It's primarily a road map not a topographical one, and, with a red ink pen, he has traced the company's journey, including dates, from its landing at Omaha Beach down to southern Normandy and across the country to Belgium.

Printed on extra-large sheets the size of the map itself, the copies are much better than I expected—the colors more vivid, the lines more distinct—and I wonder if the printer, noting the map's age, has adjusted the ink levels. Only the folds, creating a sort of creased windowpane across the map, compromise the clarity. Even the red line meandering through the countryside is visible. I also scanned and printed copies of the war journal, a dark green ledger book with accountant's lines and columns on the inside pages. Its opening sheets list every man in "HQ" Company—Headquarters Company, our father's unit—and includes Social Security numbers, ranks, hometowns, and dates of injuries or death or, in some cases, battle fatigue. The daily journal account begins on page twenty-five, the day they left the United States headed to Europe. It's a momentous day, and in capital letters with bold, thick blue ink that has not faded through the years, my father has written, "1944 Feb. 13—Left point of embarkation, Boston Mass, aboard U.S.S. Argentina."

Edwin and Ellen have not seen the journal in years, not since we were children playing in the basement, and, like me back then, they never paid attention to it; probably not one of us had read its pages or knew what information was inside. When I hand them the stapled copies, thirty pages front and back of a year of war, they receive the pages silently, as if they are precious documents seen for the first time. I give them a minute to take in the familiar handwriting, as I have already done, and place themselves in a different time and country.

Most of the writing follows liberations of towns, from Isigny to Mortain, eventually leading to what our father called the "rat race" through France into Belgium after the Battle of Normandy. The map ends at the French and Belgian border. We'll need other historical records to fill in the rest of the 1944–45 journey.

Ellen has collected Europe planning maps for each of us at the Greensboro AAA office. We open the modern map of France, looking for the same highways that connect Omaha Beach to Saint-Lô, to Domfront, to Mortain. The contemporary route is the same, meandering south as it once did, passing through village after village. We can follow this road exactly as he did.

While we plot map lines upstairs, Bill waits downstairs, reading, straightening bookshelves, loading the crockpot with beef and vegetables that will become dinner. I can hear the chattering of sports commentators doing play-by-play on a baseball game, plates and silverware clinking as he empties the dishwasher and clears breakfast dishes. From the upstairs window, I watch his car ease out of the driveway and return thirty minutes later.

I wanted him to join us upstairs. After all, he's going on this trip, too, I reminded him. He knows what I want from it, and he knows my concerns. Still unsure of my authority with Edwin and Ellen, I'd love his input and presence.

"I'm just tagging along," he said over coffee that morning. Saturday's newspaper was open on the table, his elbow pressing an indentation into today's below-the-fold story. He could sit for hours on weekends, reading through articles and refilling his cup. Early sun dappled the headlines, and he looked over the top of his glasses. "Anyway, it's your father, they're your brother and sister."

"But we wanted to do this ourselves, without them. I still want to do it the way we planned."

"It's taken on a life of its own, hasn't it?" His blue eyes were clear. "But it can still be the trip we wanted. We'll make sure of that."

I sighed, shook my head.

"You have to stand your ground," he said. "Don't let them take it over."

"I'll do my best," I said. He is the oldest of four boys, and he assumes the leadership role among his siblings in much the same way as Edwin once did in my family. I can't imagine his youngest brother, born ten years after Bill, taking charge of the three older brothers.

At a few minutes after noon, we three plus Bill head for lunch at a local barbecue restaurant, famous for its chopped pork shoulders. Over sandwiches and red slaw, we talk about our children, family, jobs.

"So far, so good," I whisper to Bill as we head back to the car. Things have gone well. Edwin and Ellen are listening, and they are adding ideas of their own. If they know how much I have worried about this meeting, how much I feared they would take it over, they don't show it.

For the next two hours after lunch, back at the house, we bend over maps, write lists, and talk through ideas. By midafternoon, our heads are spinning with details. We divide responsibilities. Ellen and I will begin searching for contacts, experts, or simply anyone willing to meet with us. Edwin plans to meet with his travel agent and investigate hotels and other arrangements. He'll get her advice on transportation across Europe for the five of us. We've selected dates—three weeks in May, not quite a year away.

Edwin says goodbye first, climbs down the stairs, and heads back to Georgia. "That went well," Ellen says as she watches him pull out of the driveway. She soon follows, maps, journal pages, a legal pad of notes, and more tucked under one arm. Highlighters, sticky and Post-it notes, and paper clips are left scattered across my upstairs coffee table.

I sit for a moment by myself, gazing out the window and watching her back onto my street and drive away. I turn out the lights, and head downstairs. At the bottom of the steps, there is Bill, holding two glasses of wine.

CHAPTER 4

I was sitting in the front seat of the Corvair, impatient to leave, when Daddy reached in the open window and pushed down the lock. "Don't want you falling out, do we?" He said that every time we drove together, and every time I rolled my eyes, knowing how easy it would be for me to lean over and pop that lock right back up if I wanted to.

What would stop me from opening the door were the poles he was lashing to the passenger side mirror and the back seat door handle that curved out from the door like a quarter moon. "A little higher," he said, and I curved my fist around the cane poles while he wrapped the twine around the mirror and the handle and tied it with a double bow we could easily untie when we got to the pond.

When I was younger, we were out almost every Saturday or Sunday, it seemed. But these days, he often didn't feel good on weekends, or he was working in the yard or at the plant. I was a budding teenager, always looking for something to do with friends. But when he was home and feeling good, and I had no other plans, and when Mama started listing chores for us both, we'd do anything to get out of the house.

"Are we ever going to use rods and reels?" I asked. He took them when he fished at the beach, but for pond fishing, we turned to bobbers and corks. He had taught me how to swing the line into the water and watch the bobber ripple to the bank. He taught me when to let the bobber bob and when to jerk the line and hook the fish. We'd have more luck, I told him, if we'd use better equipment.

"A fish doesn't care what kind of stick we're holding," he always said. I suspected our fishing Saturdays weren't so much about catching fish for him, and maybe they weren't for me either. He tucked his tackle box into the rear seat floorboard, slid into position in front, double-checked the glove compartment for the Maalox bottle, rolled his window all the way down, lit a cigarette, and we were off, backwards down the curving driveway bordered by the brick wall that my grandfather had hit a dozen times, turning right on Ridgecrest, down to Worth, and, soon, to the edge of town, where he pulled up in front of the usual curb market, white chipping paint, two gas pumps outside. "Fattest, juiciest worms in the county," he said. A few years back when I was younger, we set up a barrel of rich dirt in the back yard and harvested our own worms that we fed with orange peels, eggshells, and other table scraps. They multiplied so quickly that soon we could scoop them out like strands of spaghetti. It was one of those good ideas that got out of control. When worms were so thick we could barely get the top back on the barrel, we dumped the whole thing into the woods behind the house and started buying worms.

I climbed over the gear shift, since I couldn't get out over the lashed poles, and followed Daddy out the driver's side door. His old Bermuda shorts were wrinkled, like he had just pulled them out of his drawer. He probably had. The green plaid shirt he was wearing had pockets in front for hooks and an occasional worm, and it was old enough he could wipe his hands across the front and Mama wouldn't mind if it didn't wash clean.

In the market, he grabbed the worm carton, a bottled Coke for himself and a Nehi grape for me, and, after paying at the cash register, chatted a few minutes with the men sitting on a bench out front while we finished our drinks. We dropped the empty bottles in the crate by the door, slid back in through the driver's side, and eased back onto the road.

"I've got a surprise for you today." He drove with his right wrist, the other arm stuck out the window, his shirt sleeve flapping.

"What is it?"

"You'll see." He turned off the two-lane highway onto a road unfamiliar to me, and he slowed. "Fella who works in shipping owns this place. Says it's stocked with bream and catfish and who knows what all. We'll haul home dinner tonight."

"Is that the surprise?"

"You'll see."

He turned in at an old wooden mailbox and steered the Corvair down a gravel road that curled clouds of dust around our windows and behind the bumper. "I think this is right. He said we'd wind a while till we get to a private driveway then follow a trail in the woods for a little ways."

His eyes were focused on the bumpy road. Pretty soon, a driveway showed up on the left and Daddy pulled the Corvair into the grass opposite. A small break in the woody growth revealed a the beginning of a trail.

It was a narrow path, lined by brush and cluttered with limbs that had fallen haphazardly, as though no one had walked through here lately. I could hear a blue gurgling, a creek or maybe even a waterfall. I followed behind Daddy, hoisting the tackle box, slapping mosquitos. He carried the worms and the poles, which kept snagging on branches. A thin trail of water now followed us on the right, growing thicker and bouncing noisily over rocks and sticks fallen in the water.

"Here we go," he said at last. We'd come to a bend in the creek. He squatted. Put his poles down on the leaves. "This is it."

"This is what?"

"Natural spring water." It was a deep pool of the clearest water I'd ever seen. It didn't flow like the creek water that surrounded it but sat in its own space in the turn of the creek. Delicate ripples patterned its surface. On a branch by the spring, a tin cup dangled by its handle. Daddy lifted it off. "It's underground water that can't go any further, so it rises to the surface." He dipped the cup, swirled it around in the water then scooped. Droplets splashed back into the pool.

"Go ahead, taste it. You won't find anything better." I put my lips to the cold cup and sipped. Fresh, clear, and ice-cold. He was right, it was really good. He laughed as he watched me gulp it down then scooped a cupful for himself. "Hard to find, natural springs like this, and when you do, you need to drink all you can. It's good for you. Pure. Will cure anything, Granny used to say. We had one down by the creek when I was a boy, and Granny would send me down to get a bucket she could sip on all day." I tried to picture my old granny at a younger age, my father as a boy.

We sat on the bank for a few minutes, trading drinks of water from the cup like we were sharing communion. It was cool back in the woods, even though it was a scorching July day. "Let's get at it," Daddy finally said, looping the cup back on the branch and pulling himself up. A black ant had made its way onto my knee. I knocked it off, stood, and caught up with Daddy as he followed the trail a little further to a clearing where, sure enough, the flow of water slowed and a good-sized pond opened up. His fella in shipping had forgotten to tell him there wasn't much clearing around the pond, so we walked through weeds halfway up my bare calves to get to the edge of the water. Mosquitos and chiggers jumped off Queen Anne's lace and chewed us up. As always, though, when we first arrived, the pond seemed full of possibilities, full of fish.

But it wasn't.

A few nibbles pulled our bobbers under, but the only thing we hauled in was a palm-sized spot whose body was so small the hook went straight through its mouths to its gills. We eased the hook out gently so as not to tear the flesh further. Daddy assured me it would heal. "Go back and grow a little bit," Daddy said. "We'll get you next time."

He could have done this all afternoon and then some. He threw his line in, leaned back on the bank, and closed his eyes. He wouldn't have known if he got a nibble or not. I was itching all over, chiggers feasting on my arms and legs. I moved down the pond, threw in, found a place in the shade, threw in again. I circled the pond this way, Daddy still tossing it in from the bank where he had begun, smoking, staring out at nothing.

"I don't think much is biting today," I finally said. We'd been there at least an hour.

"Giving up so soon?"

We rarely caught anything, that was the thing. Time after time, it was the same. Next Saturday, or the next or the next, whenever Daddy got a break from the plant, whenever Mama came at me with housework to do, we'd be at it again like a couple of fugitives, windows down, poles lashed to the car handles, carton of worms in the back seat, driving and driving through the country, it didn't matter where, no better way to spend an afternoon.

CHAPTER 5

My trip research begins in earnest in the weeks that follow our first sibling meeting. Two times in his journal, our father mentions "an old monastery in Kerkrade," and once "an old monastery in Germany." I type "old monastery in Kerkrade" into the Google search bar. The first entry takes me to the website of a twelfth-century abbey, called Rolduc, right on the Netherlands–Germany border. I can't say for certain, but I feel this must be the monastery he's referring to. How many could there be? Perhaps a lot, I think, in a country so rich with history. Earlier I feared the abbey, if it still existed, would be in ruins, a crumbling place not fit for tourists, but I've underestimated medieval architecture and the European talent for historical preservation. The Rolduc Abbey flourished in the decades leading into the twenty-first century. Today it thrives as a conference center, hotel, and restaurant.

On Sunday evening, I click the email link on the website and send a message to the anonymous recipient, explaining our plan, asking for advice or help. When I hit "send," I feel as if I am tossing a bottle into an ocean with a hopeful but unlikely chance the bottle will ever be found.

Monday morning begins as usual with the scent of cinnamon bagels lingering throughout the house. In the kitchen, the coffee pot is down to its lukewarm half cup. My first class at the university is not until eleven, so I linger over morning news before opening my laptop and scrolling through messages, deleting the usual junk and sending quick replies to students. At the bottom of the unread emails, there it is: a reply from rolduc.com, no longer an anonymous correspondence but a message from a person named Enrique Martens.

Bill has just stepped from the shower, wrapped only in a towel. I race from the kitchen to the bedroom where he's reaching for a pair of khakis.

"Listen: 'This is the place where US soldiers stayed during the war.'" I pause. "I just emailed them last night, and already a response."

"This is the monastery?" Bill turns from the mirror to face me. "Go on."

I continue reading as he dresses: "'We are now a hotel, and when you come here, you can stay in the rooms where the troops stayed. In addition, I can arrange a tour of the abbey for you and your family when you visit.'" I pause and look up. "We have our first place to stay, our first contact. And a tour!"

Bill slides his arms into his shirt sleeves and fastens the buttons. "Wow, that's exciting."

I forget about time and my students anticipating my arrival at the university. Back in the kitchen, I phone Ellen and, when she doesn't answer, I leave a message. "Call me. I've got some news." Edwin picks up immediately. He's in the middle of a dog walk in downtown Augusta.

"We're really going to do this, aren't we?" he says.

"We need more, but this is a good start."

"That's fabulous," Ellen says when she calls an hour later. "I'm going to start researching tonight, as soon as I get home from work."

Photographs of the abbey on the website show it as an architectural beauty with its original twelfth-century stone walls and bell tower. Newer construction, from the sixteenth century, includes the chapel and library. Rooms, once used as dormitories for young friars and later student priests and, during the war, for American soldiers, surround a lush grass courtyard which is divided by symmetrical diamonds in lines as precise as those of the men who once stood in formation on those grounds.

As I read its history, I picture young cleric Ailbertus settling into the small wooden chapel on the Würm River that would become the abbey. I imagine young priests, including the two who, frustrated by the strict lifestyle, attempt to destroy the abbey by setting it on fire. Young Catholic school boys roam the hallways. Soldiers in wartime, so far from home and weary with the daily realities of death, find a good night's sleep within these walls. And there, in my imagination, is my father, relaxing with a hot meal and perhaps a cold beer or a glass of wine as if he were on holiday and not marching into Hitler's failing Reich.

An hour later, I fly into my classroom just as students are checking their watches and considering leaving. Later that evening, I send more emails, this time to government offices in Barenton, Domfront, and Mortain.

I don't have to wait long until the second confirmation arrives.

"Dear Mrs. Presnell, we received your message and we would be honored to welcome you in Mortain next year." Sonia Leprovost, the secretary to the mayor of Mortain, France, explains that when an American veteran or their families visit, the city likes to organize a reception at the town hall. "We will contact Mr. Charles Lebrun too. He is living in Mortain and will be happy to meet you and share experiences. He was a young man in 1944 and remembers well what happened."

Again, I share my news with Bill. "Someone who was there when it happened. And a reception. Can you imagine? It's like we are the heroes just by being children of a soldier." I forward the email to Edwin and Ellen. "More success!" I write. "Two stops now!"

Buoyed by the responses to my initial inquiries, I send emails to villages all over France and the Netherlands that are named in the journal. Ellen also is filling up her outbox with queries to mayors of towns in Belgium and Germany.

Enrique Martens at the Rolduc Abbey puts me in touch with a local historian in Kerkrade who knows a guy in Belgium who can show me around the countryside and many battle sights. In this way, one link at a time, I build my chain of contacts. The network of 30th Infantry Division enthusiasts turns out to be much larger than I had imagined.

More stops on our tour are lined up with people I've met online who are excited to show us around and tell us their stories. With each one, I email Edwin and Ellen: "Got one! That's three stops. Got another one!"

Still, we have gaps. No one in the Rhine River region has responded, and we need someone on the Elbe River who can help us. We can't solidify travel plans until we have a working itinerary that will carry us across western Europe, from Normandy to Saxony-Anhalt.

In early August, frustrated by dead ends, I return to the 30th Infantry Division website, designed and maintained by Frank Towers. a ninety-year-old veteran from the 30th Infantry Division with a sharp memory for detail. His site is a gold mine in many ways, filled with history, personal memories, photographs, and data from battles that helps me connect my father's records with historical accounts. Towers has written articles about the soldiers' movements across France and into Germany, filling in weeks that were gaps in our father's accounting.

He details battles in chronological order. In addition to his own articles, he's encouraged other veterans to add their experiences, and many have contributed.

Some of Towers's history coincides exactly with our father's experience, but a lot of it does not. For example, Towers describes in detail the liberation of prisoners on a train near Magdeburg, Germany, bound for the Theresienstadt concentration camp in Czechoslovakia where they would likely have been exterminated, but the incident is not included in our father's journal. Surely if Daddy had come that close to the horrific operation of the Holocaust, he would have recorded it. He didn't.

I decide to write to Towers. "Here's what we're doing," I say in a short email describing our plans and desires. "We're having trouble finding contacts. Can you help?"

His answer, a full two pages, written with the same detail I read on his website, arrives the next morning—his words are clear, vivid, and informative.

He begins, "I knew your father. He was in the 117th regiment with me."

No, my father's HQ Company was in the 120th not the 117th, though both, plus the 119th, were regiments of the 30th Infantry Division. The rest of his email both confirms and conflicts with what we know of our father's journey. I appreciate Towers's quick and friendly response, but something is off. I respond, suggesting he remembers the wrong soldier.

Towers sends another email almost immediately. "Maybe, but I don't think so. Here's what I have." He gives information on name, rank, and more. Everything he says fits.

"We have your father as being in the 120th regiment but also in the 117th," he says, "but I can correct that based on your information." He explains that the three regiments were always within five miles of each other, which might explain the different data. He also includes the regiments' movements after victory was declared, which my father's journal left untold, as well as the possibility that many soldiers from the 120th were reassigned to the 117th after the war. It sounds like a possible explanation, enough to convince me that his memories must be of my father, in spite of the years that have passed.

Then he adds: "I believe that I have a photo of your father, meeting up with the Russians. Small world! The photo isn't labeled, so I'm going on memory, but I'm pretty sure this is Sgt. Presnell. I will send it to you!"

Not possible, I think. Seventy-five years have passed since the war. With no label, that soldier could be anybody, and it is more than unlikely to be my father.

The following night an email arrives with the subject line, "Photo," and a single attachment. Shaking my head, I click on the link and wait for the image to open. It takes a minute for it to load on my old desktop, similar to waiting for a Polaroid film to magically reveal a captured face.

Suddenly, there is my father—twenty-nine years old, healthy and strong, looking right at me, in a photograph as distinct and vivid as if it were just snapped with a digital camera. In the black-and-white image, he stands between two Soviet soldiers, both shorter than he is by several inches, and his arms hang loosely around their shoulders. They wear heavy overcoats to his light jacket, caps to his helmet. Around his neck, a camera dangles from a leather cord. In the background, an overpass curves above the highway to the left and a small hill rises up on the right. My father is holding the stub of a cigar between the fingers of his left hand.

I know the day, because in his album are two full pages of photos he took of that day, of groups of soldiers and officers from both armies, photos he has labeled simply, "Ruskies." It is April 25, 1945, a day of celebration. American soldiers have crossed the river to shake hands with the Soviets in a historic moment that symbolizes the inevitable end of German domination across Europe.

Unlike the photos in his album which are faded and scratched from years, this one is undamaged, as though it has been stored somewhere, away from light, preserved, perhaps, since the war.

I lean in closer, and now a fourteen-year-old me meets young Bill Presnell's eyes. For more than forty years, I've longed for him, missed him, hated him, tried to forget him, and for that many years, he has remained as essential to me as my arms, my feet, my beating heart. I've looked for him in the cemetery, on cold nights, lying in the grass, my fist around a near-empty bottle of wine. I've smoked his brand of cigarettes as though, genie-like, he'd swirl up from the clouds and take me in his arms. I've gone fishing with my uncle Tom, pretending it's the same, though it never is.

Those years when I was living at home and my mother asked me to clean the gutters of our family home, I climbed a ladder to the roof and sat beside the cupola, looking across town to where the bank building and the First Methodist Church steeple rose above the other structures, and I imagined him gazing at the same buildings years before. I studied the photographs of him we took back then, sitting in his coat and tie on my grandparents' steps, standing on top of Grandfather Mountain beside my mother, holding my sister's hand in our snowy front yard. I turned him into characters in my stories and poems.

But the young man in the photograph is not yet my father. His face, even in the shadow of his helmet, is smooth like a boy's. He's thinner than I've ever seen him, younger, and here, even after this year of war, his eyes seem full of possibility. I've seen only one other photo of him before he was my father, one I found in the county library—a high school graduation picture in which he's staring off at something outside the camera view while his classmates watch the photographer, as though his mind is far from this place, perhaps wondering what in the world he will do now. Five years later, he would join the National Guard. Five years after that, he'd find himself here on the bank of the Elbe. Ten years later, he'd have a daughter named Barbara.

This new photograph is so real I can feel the wind rising off the waters of the Elbe, I can breathe in the sweet cigar smoke. The helmet on his head is the same one stored now in a box in my attic, the same one I set precariously on my own head as far back as I can remember and as recently as a week ago, as though in wearing it I would know his thoughts and find myself in them. The uniform he wears might be the exact same one that's hanging now in my closet.

I'm coming, I say to the picture, to the young man who will be my father. Your daughter, who never had a chance to tell you good-bye, is on her way to you.

CHAPTER 6

March in the South is transition season. A stretch of blue sky and teasing sun—false springs, my grandmother called them—might shift at the snap of a finger to heavy snow and cold that can linger for a week. Growing up, we'd long for this last burst of winter when we could wax up the sled runners and add one more snow day to the school year. These are wet snows, soon reduced to mud dried up by another burst of sun when early jonquils and crocuses pop out of the ground. The weather lies this time of year, telling early flowers it's safe, and then cackling with laughter when, a few days later, the blossoms wilt with frost.

On the first day of March in 1969, nine inches of snow fell on already warm earth. By the next day, most of the accumulation had turned to slush. The world was damp but not cold—cloudy, gray, and dispirited.

On Monday after the Saturday snowstorm, Daddy checked into the hospital for surgery on an ulcerated stomach. All the Maalox in the world would not soothe his pain away, and he couldn't keep food down. A few years back a surgeon had removed a different ulcer, but this new one was larger, more problematic. "A third of your stomach will need to go," I recall somebody said.

Months earlier, the plant owner, Mr. Stedman, had promoted him—though my mother insisted it was no promotion. Rather than supervise operations on the T-shirt plant just a few blocks from home, he would locate in Lumberton and Red Springs in the eastern part of the state to help open textile mills that would manufacture T-shirts for the army. No, he wouldn't have to move. It was temporary placement, Mondays through Fridays for a while.

"Tell him you just won't go anymore," I overheard Mama tell Daddy one Friday night after he'd been making the weekly trek for several months. Travel and a steady diet of restaurant food had already begun to aggravate his tender stomach. "Your body can't take much more. Hasn't the mill taken enough?"

I didn't hear his reply, but on Monday morning, just like every Monday morning, he got in the car, headed east, and didn't come home until Friday.

Mama told us that even from his hospital bed the night before surgery, he reached into the nightstand drawer for a cigarette. For the thousandth time, she urged him to stop. "Can't you see what it's doing to you?" I imagined her saying. He was a two-pack-a-day man, a habit he acquired, as with many men of his generation, in the army. He was never without those Winstons in his front shirt pocket.

The Tuesday surgery was successful, but on Wednesday night, something went wrong. I don't know what happened, and I don't remember ever being told. What I do remember is my mother later that morning, standing in the hallway of the hospital with the surgeon, distraught and angry, and the surgeon cowered.

Thursday morning, I woke to hear Daddy Bunting, my maternal grandfather, calling my name. Before we headed to school, he told me, we were going to the hospital to see Daddy. My mother was already there. Our father had fallen into a coma, was not responding to medications, and the numbers on his machines were declining rapidly, he told me in his soft voice.

Daddy Bunting was the kindest, gentlest man I knew. He wore a three-piece suit with a white shirt and tie no matter what time of day. This morning, even as early as it was, he was perfectly dressed, which was oddly comforting. He was the one who, a few years before, met us children at the house after school on the day President Kennedy was assassinated. He didn't want us to be alone, waiting for our parents to come home from work. Later, he was the one we spent a summer with while my mother was in graduate school, and my grandmother worked the day shift at the hospital. He'd mix us tomato juice with fresh tomatoes from the garden, would walk us to the Jitterburger grill for lunch. Later still, he was the one sitting in the living room watching *General Hospital* when Ellen and I arrived home from school every afternoon.

Mama Bunting, my maternal grandmother, was a nurse and a woman who gave orders and did not take them. She probably sent my grandfather that Thursday morning, so she could join my mother at the hospital. "Bring them here, and then get them to school," I could imagine her saying. "They might as well be in class."

Daddy Bunting didn't talk much, most likely because he didn't hear well, but I listened when he spoke. This morning, he barely touched my shoulder. He didn't turn on my lamp, but the hallway light cast a yellow glow across my blanket.

Across the hall, my sister Ellen's light was on, and I heard her dresser drawers opening and closing. I didn't hear her crying, but it was possible Daddy Bunting urged her not to cry for my sake. He scrambled eggs and made toast. We ate quickly, gathered our books, and left.

One at a time, we were allowed to visit Daddy's hospital room. When it was my turn, I found him hooked to machines that pumped and hissed. He was pale, his eyes closed, his skin cold when I touched his hand. I opened and closed the drawer beside his bed to see the pack of cigarettes Mama said was there. I told him he needed to get well, because I'd found a new pond for us to fish. I didn't get a response, just the beep beep of machines and my father's closed eyes, his face oddly peaceful.

Ellen and I arrived at school in time for second period. By then, our teachers had learned that our father was critical, and they accepted us back into class without question or tardy slip. Somehow, my classmates had gotten the word, too. I walked into algebra—my teacher was Mrs. Craven, and she and my mother shared rides every week to Greensboro for graduate school courses—and the entire class hushed as I tucked my head down and watched my feet moving across the floor and between desks to my spot at the back of the classroom. I slid low into my seat and felt all eyes on me. For the rest of the day, nobody talked to me, as if they got too close, they'd catch what I had.

My mother hadn't told my brother about my father's surgery because she didn't want to complicate, even for a day, his fragile academic life. The previous fall he had been home from college on academic suspension because during his freshman year he had partied more than he studied. He then found a job hauling equipment and running errands for a surveying company. In January my parents sent him back to school with a laundry list of "you will or else" expectations, and barely two months into the new semester he was struggling.

When he got the call that Thursday morning in his dorm room, he threw a duffle bag of clothes together and hurried to the nearest highway to hitch a ride home from Clemson, in upstate South Carolina, a four-hour drive in light traffic. He was at the hospital by midafternoon, at my mother's side and beside my father's bed. Already he had assumed the role of man of the house.

Friday morning at four o'clock, my bedroom was dark, except for a faint glow from a lamp spilling in from Ellen's room. Again, I felt a soft hand rocking my shoulder. "Barbara? Barbara?" The voice behind the whisper was familiar. I looked out from beneath my blanket so I could see the face.

"It's Mrs. Chandler," the voice said. "Mullie Chandler." I sat up, remembering that my mother had asked her to stay over that night with Ellen and me. She was in my parents' bridge club, though she was a few years older with almost grown children. Her hair spun off the back of her head in a perfect beehive, and her sweet milky eyes were shadowed in the scant light of the room. As sleepy as I was, I knew that something must be terribly wrong, or Mrs. Chandler would not be shaking my shoulder in the darkness.

"I need you to get up," she said. "I'm going to take you to the hospital." The silver twist of her hair was haloed by faint light. I saw the shadow of Ellen walking to the bathroom, snuffing up tears. I didn't say anything but removed the covers and quietly slid into the dress I had laid out on a chair the night before. When both of us were ready, we followed Mrs. Chandler to the carport where her Buick had pulled into the space my mother's car usually occupied, right beside Daddy's Corvair. We followed the streetlights to the hospital. Mrs. Chandler reached for my hand as we walked to the hospital building, but I pulled away. Ellen held on tightly to me, and I let her.

We found my mother sitting in the hospital chapel with our minister. She motioned for us to sit beside her, and she gripped my hand with hers. She didn't have to say anything for us to know that it was all over.

At six o'clock that morning, Edwin, Ellen, and I rode back to our house with Mrs. Chandler, and Mama stayed at the hospital to sign papers and take care of business. It was still dark outside, and Ellen and I were sent back to bed, but Edwin sat up in the living room, talking with Mrs. Chandler, whose youngest child, Billy, was a good friend of Edwin's. I wanted to be with them. I'm not sleepy, I insisted, but I was sent to my room anyway, so they could talk. Maybe they had a conversation in mind not suitable for a fourteen-year-old who just lost her father but necessary for the oldest child, the only son. Or maybe Mrs. Chandler was just there to listen. Both make sense to me now, but at the time, I felt shut out, unheard. In my room, I lay on the bed in the dark, listening to their voices murmuring in the den, but I couldn't understand their words. I didn't sleep. Instead, I lay awake in my room, the earliest morning light seeping through the curtains, my clock radio set to the local AM station, and I listened to the morning programming—the news, the weather, the obituary column on the air, George Beverly Shea singing "Ave Maria," same as every morning, same as if this were just another day.

Friday passed in a blur, like I was watching my life on fast-forward. Ellen and I didn't go to school, and at first it felt like a sick day at home. We watched *I Love Lucy* and *The Dick Van Dyke Show* reruns on television just as we did when we were home with the flu. After lunch the preacher came, and people begin to arrive, bringing pies and casseroles. After school let out Ellen's friends knocked on the door. My new friend Carol, who lived a block away, came with her parents in the late afternoon. We sat together on my bed, but neither of us spoke until she said, "I think my parents are probably ready to go." I didn't know until years later that Friday, March 7, the day my father died, was also Carol's birthday.

The next morning, Saturday, by the time I woke up and made my way to the kitchen, a coffee pot that made twenty-five cups had been set up on the counter in front of Mama's recipe box, probably by the church ladies sitting at the kitchen table with my brother. The whole house smelled of fresh coffee.

Edwin rose from the table, poured himself a fresh cup. "If I drink much more, I'm going to turn into a coffee bean." A ripple of soft laughter from the two church women and Joe, the Air Force captain now dentist from across the street who entered the kitchen from the dining room. Joe put a tray of chicken on the table, said,

"Damn it, I won't get used to it." He wiped his hands on his pants leg and then dabbed his eye with his shirtsleeve. "Germans couldn't get him, but this damn little ulcer did. A hell of a thing."

A tray of cold cuts sat to the left of the sink, still wrapped in plastic, and a box of doughnuts, the glaze stiff but the dough soft as if they'd just come from the shop, lay open beside it. The refrigerator was stuffed with pies, spaghetti casserole, Jell-O salad, ham biscuits. Last night we laid all the food out on the table, and everybody filled their plates with what they wanted. I didn't want anything but a ham biscuit and a scoop of potato salad. What I really wanted was to be in my room by myself, playing the Beatles' "Yesterday" over and over on my record player, but Mama said that wasn't polite and people wanted to see me.

Earlier that morning, Margaret from next door, so familiar to us it was as if she was part of the family, had delivered a bowl of her famous chicken salad. She'd been over about fifteen times since yesterday, but I didn't get tired of seeing her. Even when she frowned, she was smiling, and there was something in her face that suggested everything might be all right. She was sitting half on, half off Mama's chair at the table talking to Ellen, her ten-year-old son, Tommy, leaning against the refrigerator, looking toward the door, ready to leave. She had made him come, but she didn't say it. What she said instead was, "Tommy wants to say something to Tina." Tina was my mother, and she hadn't yet come out of her bedroom.

When I peeked in on my way to the kitchen, my mother was sitting at her dressing table, still wearing her thin pink bathrobe over her nightgown, her dark hair shooting out in all directions, looking into the mirror with her sad, brown eyes, as though she didn't recognize the person she saw.

"Go on back," Edwin said, and Margaret and Tommy did. They returned to the kitchen five minutes later, and Tommy headed straight out the carport door, leaving his mother in the kitchen to say she'd check in later to see if we needed anything.

Edwin had taken charge of my family, and it was reassuring to have somebody who would tell me what I was supposed to do and how I was supposed to feel because I didn't have a clue. Sometimes I'd see my brother deep in conversation with an adult who'd pulled him aside to say something, as though my brother, too, was now an adult. Nobody was pulling me aside. Not Ellen either. She sat in the rocker in the den, went to the front door whenever the doorbell rang. I wanted to be in the kitchen if Edwin was there, but I tucked into the corner next to the pantry, out of sight.

Joe came over and put his hand on Edwin's shoulder, said, "You call me if there's anything I can do." Margaret and Tommy had both gone now, and the church ladies had gotten up and were making their way toward the door.

I kept an eye on Edwin. He glanced over at me where I was standing by the stove, holding a coffee cup, getting ready to fill it, even though I didn't drink coffee. He set his cup on the counter, steam rising from the milky brew.

He pushed up the cuff of his blue sweater, rubbed his hand around his wrist the way Daddy used to when his eczema itched, and then tugged his sweater sleeve down. Now he was looking straight at me. "I want you to know that I'm going to be here for you now. Whatever you need, I don't care if I'm at Clemson or at home, you let me know. I promise."

Not for a minute could I recognize this as the brother I used to take bubble baths with, ride bikes with, or play baseball with in the yard. Nor was it the brother who a few months ago was a rejected college student trying to figure his life out. This was my brother who was going to take care of me—man of the house, no longer just a son. I believed he was capable of all that because I needed to. To have him so near eased the stabbing pains streaking through me.

He stepped closer, took the cup from my hand, said, "Want some coffee?" I didn't nod, didn't say no. He filled the cup, a little more than halfway, and he said, "You want cream, don't you?"

The back door slammed as somebody came in and, I could tell by the sound of their steps, somebody else behind them. "Yoohoo."

"In here," Edwin said, handed me my cup, and stepped to the doorway to greet whoever it was, tossing a smile back at me.

On Sunday rain came—not a refreshing spring shower but a wintry insult. That afternoon, the First Methodist Church sanctuary was packed. Both the downstairs and the balcony pews were full, and people were standing along the back wall and gathered at the door of the narthex. Ellen's friends, the McCauleys, all seven of them including their parents, sat in the first row upstairs. My Girl Scout troop squeezed together on the front pew by the altar. When the organ stopped playing, and everyone stood, my family marched down the aisle between the pews to the front row, Edwin holding tight to Mama's arm. To put us at ease Edwin whispered back to me and Ellen, "Think of it as just like every other Sunday when we come in late." When we sang, "O God Our Help in Ages Past," Edwin looked over at Ellen and then at me and smiled, as if to say, "Everything is going to be all right."

The minister, who knew Daddy's war story, described Cornelius Ryan's book *The Last Battle*, the book Daddy claimed as his own story, and said this moment, this surgery, was Daddy's last battle. He had a copy of the book at the pulpit—maybe it was Daddy's from the shelf in the den or maybe he got it from the public library. Then he mentioned Daddy's Purple Heart and Bronze Star, but he saved all the sentimental words about how we'd go on without him for the prayer, as Mama had asked him to do. A few of Daddy's army buddies gathered in the narthex, wearing their Old Hickory tie pins and some their American Legion hats. People from the mill were here, too—I saw Mr. and Mrs. Stedman, the owners; Wilbur, Daddy's friend in sales; Bob Crowley and his wife; and Mrs. Steed who worked in the office. A group of women from sewing sat together and others I recognized from first shift. Machines didn't run on Sundays, so everybody who wanted to be here could be, and it looked like a lot of them came.

We rode in the black funeral-home car across town to Oaklawn Cemetery where my parents had recently bought plots, thinking they would have many years before the spaces would be needed. I remembered two years earlier when we rode in the same car from Asheboro to East Bend, an hour away, to bury Daddy's mother, Granny, who died at age ninety-four, though senility took her mind years before. My father sat in the back seat and cried all the way to the grave site.

Mr. Stedman was waiting at the curb when we stepped out of the car. "He should never have died," he said and took Mama's hand. She half smiled and gently tugged her hand away.

It was bone cold, not in the temperature, which hovered above freezing, but in that way the cold can seep in through clothes and skin until we feel it in our marrow. We followed pallbearers carrying the casket through wet grass to the open grave. My sister's face streaked with tears, which she wiped with a tissue she pulled from her coat pocket. Mama glanced over, and I saw that her eyes were shadowed and her face pinched, as though she was holding something back. I tugged my brown Chesterfield coat around me. My coat was heavier than the temperature required, but I wanted its woolly comfort wrapping my body. I pulled my collar around my neck and leaned against Ellen. Edwin held Mama's arm, loosening his grip only when the honor guard captain presented her with the folded American flag.

Back at home, food covered every countertop and table, and family members—cousins, aunts, and uncles—as well as neighbors and church people took every seat in the kitchen or den and spilled over into the living room, which we mostly used for occasions like this. I was expected to stay and talk to the adults and show them how well I was doing, but I sneaked to my room and crouched on the floor between my bed and the window, hidden there.

By the time Ellen pushed open the door and flicked on the overhead light, darkness had arrived. Sunday night meant Methodist Youth Fellowship. Ellen loved it because those were her best friends. They weren't mine, and I didn't want to go, but a few minutes later, I was in the back seat of the Corvair, Edwin driving, headed to church. I spent the next hour and a half taking small bites of the Hardee's Husky we were served for dinner and staring silently and inattentively at the speaker throughout the whole program.

Later that night, when the house was quiet, and no one was heading up the walk with a casserole or vase of flowers, Mama lingered in the kitchen, shuffling plates of food from the counter to the refrigerator and wiping up crumbs from the counter. Ellen followed Mama's instructions, covering open containers with lids or foil, and Edwin dropped down at the kitchen table and sat for what must have been the first time in two days. I didn't know what to do, so I straddled the doorway to the den and began inching toward my bedroom.

"I need to talk with you three now that we're alone," Mama finally said, her voice hoarse. She eyed the limp dishrag, glanced over at Edwin, and then turned her eyes back to the countertop. Darkness poured in the kitchen window, and beyond the den only a faint glow shined from lights left on in the back bedrooms.

Too weary for questions, we fell in line behind her to Ellen's room where we could gather in soft lamplight. Even Edwin, now showing fatigue, dragged, following last and not speaking. Mama sat, her back straight, on the pillow end of my sister's twin bed, the one that had been mine until I moved into my own room four years earlier. The beam from the nightstand shade cast downward.

Edwin stood by the bedpost as though he needed something to steady himself until Mama said, "Sit down, Edwin," and, sliding his hand down the post, he dropped onto the bed's edge. Mama was still wearing her funeral dress, black and pencil thin, with delicate pearls around her neck. She looked beautiful, like Jackie Kennedy, I thought; an elegant widow. Dark moons around her eyes told a harsher story.

Ellen and I chose opposite beds, facing each other. I fixed my gaze on the blue shag carpet and the hemmed edge of the flowered bed skirt, looking anywhere except my mother's dark eyes. Her long fingers traced the stitching on my sister's spread.

"Things have changed for us," she began. I caught myself looking at her before I shot my gaze back down to my brown loafers. "But we'll be fine. We'll go on with our lives as usual. Ellen and Barbara, you can stay home from school tomorrow, but on Tuesday, you should go back."

Ellen and I traded glances. I didn't want to go back to school, not tomorrow, not Tuesday, not ever. Ellen started to speak, but Mama cut her off. "There's nothing for you to do here. I'll stay home this week to take care of matters, but then I'll go back to teaching next week. Edwin, I'd like you to stay a few days, if you can, but then get back to Clemson. I don't want you to sacrifice your grades over this."

"I'll stay as long as you want," he said, looking down.

"You know what your daddy wanted, for you to do well and finish at Clemson."

He nodded, scratching the knee of his pants as though a spot lingered there. I didn't see a stain, but his fingernail moved back and forth, making a faint scritch-scritch.

"Edwin is now the man of the house," she continued. "That's what your daddy would have wanted. Ellen and Barbara, you will help me take care of things, doing what your daddy would have done to the extent you can. Life will be different, but we will be fine. We don't need to dwell on this, we don't need to fall apart. We are strong. We will move on."

She paused. It was remarkable to me that she wasn't crying, though her brown eyes were hazy and distant, as if she wasn't here, sitting on the edge of the bed, as if none of this had happened, and I'd wake up tomorrow morning to Daddy's runny scrambled eggs.

"I know you loved your daddy, and he loved you," she continued. "I'm not saying it will be easy. But we won't make it any easier by going on and on about it, especially in front of others. We'll pull ourselves together."

I didn't know how to attend school on Tuesday and pretend nothing had happened. Everybody would stare at me, because they'd know, but they wouldn't say anything. I didn't know how I would get to school in the mornings without Daddy driving me on his way to work. Or how to go to sleep at night knowing he wasn't asleep in the recliner, a book in his lap. Ellen would be fine. She'd nestle in the comfort of her friends and school. Edwin would be fine. He'd buck up, go back to South Carolina, and do what Daddy wanted.

"Do you understand me, children?" she asked.

Ellen began to sniff back tears.

I looked to my mother for further instructions on how to live as she expected, but her face offered none. I didn't know what to do, but she was my mother, my only parent now, if I didn't count Edwin, and she knew best. We wouldn't talk about him again. We'd move on. We were strong that way. We'd show everyone how fine we would be.

By Tuesday, when Ellen and I returned to school, skies had returned to blue and daytime temperatures began to climb toward the seventies, much too high for March. Pink, red, and white azaleas Daddy had planted along the front of the house and beside the driveway wall began to burst from their buds, erupting out of season. So many people had sent azalea bushes as memorial gifts that a few weeks later, Mama had a bed for them built in the front yard, a dozen azaleas, all colors, just outside her bedroom window where she could see them every morning when the sun came up, every evening as she closed her curtains. Their twenty-two-year marriage had ended; their love for one another never would.

CHAPTER 7

On the morning of May 7, 2014, four of us check in at Piedmont International Airport in Greensboro, North Carolina, a small airport with one terminal and two concourses. We're late, delayed by slow packing and last-minute forgetfulness. Ellen, Bill, and I have passed through scanners at the security gate and are slipping our feet back into shoes when I hear David, Ellen's husband, call her name. His voice sounds urgent, and David is rarely urgent. I look around. We don't have time for problems.

His backpack is open on the countertop, its contents spilling out like exposed secrets. In the TSA worker's palm is a knife with a five-inch blade, polished and catching the light from the nearby window. Normally a man of few words, David is talking fast, but I hear only bits of his chatter. "I forgot it was in there. I'm a collector. I was showing my son-in-law." His hand gestures and facial expressions tell the story: he's caught, nervous, irritated, embarrassed.

The officer gives David two choices: give up the knife or get somebody to pick it up. "You're not taking it on the plane." David doesn't hesitate. He snatches his phone from the security basket and punches in his daughter Laura's number. "Get over here fast," he tells her. Her house is less than a mile away, and parking for this small airport is just outside the terminal, so she'll be able to rush in and meet him quickly. It's a good solution, if Laura comes immediately.

"We're heading to the gate," Ellen tells him. "We'll try to get them to hold the doors for you."

The plane has boarded by the time we race to the empty waiting area, and clerks are calling names of missing passengers over the speaker.

"My husband's on his way," Ellen says. "He'll be here any minute."

The clerks check their watches, disappear down the ramp to the plane, and return to the desk, throwing glances our way. The one in charge said, "Ma'am, you need to board now. We're closing the doors."

This is it, I think, pushing forward to board without Ellen. This trip I've dreamed of for over two years, that we planned for a year, this trip I detailed from train stops to meals to the half dozen people who promised to meet us, all of this is about to derail because of Ellen's husband, David. Bill and I can leave without them both, and they can catch up in Paris or not at all. Right now, I don't care.

It seems we've been waiting forever, the clerks now pacing in front of the boarding ramp, mumbling together and casting looks our way. I imagine the impatience of passengers inside, wondering why the flight is delayed. I see David heading our way, not hurrying, his backpack strapped across his shoulders. "You know what I forgot?" he says. "My neck pillow."

"Come on!" Ellen says. He hustles to the ramp, and doors close behind him, as impatient passengers watch us stuff backpacks into the overhead bin, crawl into the only empty seats, and buckle up for takeoff.

I pull out my phone to power it down for the flight when a text from Edwin pops onto my screen: "Stuck in Charlotte. Mechanical delay. I don't know any more except I'm tired of waiting. I have no idea when we'll leave or if I'll make my connection in New York."

His plan has been to join the rest of us in the Paris airport where we'd grab a meal and then separate for two days until we would gather in Caen to begin our family journey. His delay is concerning, but I've made enough international flights to know it's not unusual.

A short layover in Atlanta, and we board our international flight without difficulty. Six hours later, we touch down at the Charles de Gaulle Airport. It's early morning on May 8, and the airport is not busy except for those on our flight passing through customs and making their way to baggage and transportation

"Any word from Edwin?" Ellen asks. "I haven't heard anything."

I turn on my phone and wait for incoming notices to arrive. "Nothing."

It's not Edwin's fault, of course. Still, I want to be with him, helping him negotiate the frustrating experience of rescheduling missed flights, just to make sure he makes it. Sure, my interest is selfish. Traveling takes patience, something I've never given Edwin much credit for having. I've never thought of him as adaptable, either. He's traveled the United States, but the only language he can speak fluently is Southern American English. I'm not sure how far his southern charm—and he has an abundance—will get him in France.

We load our bags into a taxi SUV and head into Paris. It should be a thirty-minute drive at most, but the closer we are to the city, the more cars, bicycles, and crowds of pedestrians scurry in all directions, jaywalking across streets, backing up traffic, until we are creeping behind slow-moving vehicles that have all but stalled in the middle of the Paris streets. Our driver reaches a set of barricades and can go no farther. He backs up, turns left, continues following side streets, then, finding himself blocked again, heads the other way. When I comment on the excessive traffic, he shakes his head.

"It's holiday," our driver explains. "Nobody works. Shops are closed. There will be parades in every arrondissement."

"What's the holiday?" I ask.

"Of course, it's VE Day. Victory in Europe. May 8. The end of the war. It's our big holiday." He tips his eyes up and catches mine in the rearview mirror.

I'm stunned. I'm embarrassed. I should have known this, should have made the connection long ago. "We don't celebrate it in America," I explain to the driver, as much as I'm trying to excuse myself. He shrugs, as though this is not something he expects Americans to know, which embarrasses me even more. I don't want to be one of those Americans.

I recall researching the day when the war came to an end, studying so many images of the streets of New York and my own hometown of Asheboro overrun with soldiers and sailors, families and friends. It was a day celebrated across the world, and yet in America today May 8 passes like any other day. No stores close their doors, no parades roll through the downtown streets in cities or small towns, stock markets remain open, mail arrives in the box right on time. It's a day no one remembers, save some aging vets who will never forget.

I apologize to the driver to make myself feel better, and then I tell our story, how we've come as siblings to follow our father's map, to find the places he fought, to imagine how he must have felt when the war was raging and when it was finally over and he could head home.

"Very, very interesting. And where is your brother, the third sibling?"

Ellen tells him about Edwin, caught somewhere in a hotel or an airport or, by now, perhaps in a plane over the ocean.

"Nothing is what we plan, is it?" He laughs and shakes his head as he eases through blockades on a side street that's closed and makes his way through crowds that spill onto both sides. Finally, he pulls the taxi in front of the Hotel Beaugency, our home for two nights. These extra days in Paris are a bonus for Ellen and David, who've never been to this city, and a gift to Bill and me, who can't get enough of it. We've been with the driver for more than an hour. With his skill navigating through street-side celebrations and traffic, plus his invaluable information, he is exactly who we needed at the wheel.

"I hope you find your brother," he says smiling, as he climbs back into his SUV after unloading our luggage.

After dropping our bags at the hotel, we find a table at a street-side café and fill up on omelets, croissants, and coffee. Shops and most restaurants are closed throughout the city in observance of the holiday. On Rue Cler, even the famous market is shut down. We walk past revelers, flags draped from buildings, and streets crowded with people.

All day, we wait for news from Edwin. "Landed in Paris at last," he writes in a text that evening. "Now to get a cab and see if my train ticket to Caen is still valid."

I'm somewhat relieved. The four of us are sitting in an outdoor café in the Marais district eating steak frites. He's hours late, but at least we're in the same country, and for a short time the same city. I'll feel better when I see him in person.

We dig into dinner and enjoy an extra bottle of wine. Afterward, we walk the lively streets of the Marais district before catching the Metro back to the Rue Cler. I'm climbing into bed when a text pops onto my screen. Edwin.

"I'm eating buffalo chicken in a little grill in Caen. Nobody speaks English and I don't speak French, but everybody speaks money." He's doing fine, he writes.

"Be careful," I write back. "And be nice."

The next morning, Ellen, David, Bill, and I board the high-speed train at the Paris Saint Lazare station. Three-plus hours later, we pull into the depot in Caen, France, and drag our luggage to the parking lot. There, in baggy khakis, an oversized shirt, and a multi-pocketed vest, stands my brother, his arms open wide, a grin across his face. I can't remember when I've been so glad to see him.

Omaha Beach, a five-mile stretch of sand, is one of five landing points where Allied troops came ashore beginning on D-Day, June 6, 1944. The beach was divided by American generals into eight segments, from Charlie on the far west end to Fox Red on the far east. Near the middle sits Easy Red, the site where tourist vans and buses unload hundreds of visitors a day, and dozens of memorials honor military units that landed there. The Normandy American Cemetery sits on a hill above it, looking down on the shoreline.

Our father, in the first entry in his journal, dated February 12, 1944, notes his voyage across the Atlantic on the USS *Argentina* to Scotland and then England, but he doesn't include details. Frank Towers on his website remembers seasick soldiers and the uneasy experience of seeing nothing but water in every direction. Daddy does describe the troops' extended stay in Southampton, England, training every day and enjoying the company of English women at night. A long gap of days and entries follows, and then, on June 12, 1944, he writes, "Crossed English Channel, arrived Omaha beachhead (Fox Red) France."

I can't wait to be standing on the sand of Omaha Beach to begin our journey, but our tour is not until this afternoon, so we drive from the train station to the Caen Memorial Museum where the most extensive collection of history and artifacts on the Omaha Beach landing is located. Sitting at the end of Esplanade Général Eisenhower, the museum is a stark, boxy building lined with the flags of the Allied powers, including the Soviet Union, a welcome yet sobering site for visitors from all countries.

Inside the museum, we grab sandwiches in the upstairs café and then split up to browse the exhibits. I begin my museum tour in the theater with a thirty-minute film on the D-Day landing. Documentary footage takes viewers back to the days leading up to that rainy June morning when young men raced through ocean waves, their rifles high in the air, to the beachheads. Black-and-white news clips, jerking and scratched, depict soldiers smoking cigarettes as they crowd on landing boats, looking out over the water, their nervous laughter erupting then quieting. Even in the warm theater of the museum, I feel the cold, my skin clammy with fear. As wave after wave of men rush into the rough water, I shiver, watching them half swim, half run, their boots filling with water, some on the last race of their lives.

Afterward, bearing an emotional weight that's difficult to carry, I find an iron bench outside the theater and sit to write—to remember and to process—in my notebook. I wonder at the miracle that any soldier—American, British, or Canadian—lived through that day. Had our father arrived on June 6 instead of six days later—a much easier landing—our story might have ended here before it ever began. Edwin walks past as I'm finishing my page. "Pretty hard stuff, isn't it?" he says. I agree.

Together we walk to the Information Desk to meet our guide, Sandrina, and join the others for our afternoon tour. Sandrina's dark hair falls below her shoulders. She was a history teacher after she first finished university, she tells us, and now loves helping visitors understand the war and its effect on the people and the landscape. Driving to the beaches in the tour van as we wind through villages, passing buildings and homes, we see American, British, and Canadian flags fluttering from windows and porches side by side with French flags.

"You see that everywhere," she says, before we ask. "People are still so grateful. The old people will tell you what it was like during occupation and how much they loved the Americans."

She's filled with stories and excited to share them. She tells us of a young man named Billy Wright, an American teenager who was the first soldier killed in a village that later honored him by naming a street after him.

"I love one story in particular," Sandrina continues as she drives. "In 2005, a soldier's body was discovered in an unmarked grave, and his seventy-nine-year-old widow came to his official burial, sixty-one years after his death, in the Normandy American Cemetery. He was from Minnesota, where she still lives. And even though she remarried and has a family now, she returns every year to pay tribute to him."

As she drives she tells more stories of men and women, ordinary French people caught up in the war, wanting to get their lives back, wanting to keep their families safe and willing to risk everything for their country. American soldiers brought hope and youth, and they weren't yet weary with defeat. The people of Normandy did everything they could to help.

Our first stop on Sandrina's tour is the German bunkers on the hillside that faced the beaches, poised for an Allied invasion. Cold concrete and steel, the fortresses even now seem impenetrable. We walk down into their cavernous rooms where I imagine German soldiers, boys themselves, yearned for home. It's cold here, dark, and today's dampness seems to seep through my shoes into my bones.

Back on the road, after a short drive, Sandrina joins other cars and tour vans en route to the parking lot of the Omaha Beach memorial site. "The beach stretches for miles in both directions," she says. "This is the segment called Easy Red."

As she wheels into one of the few vacant parking spaces, I lean forward and ask, "How far is Fox Red from here?" From our maps, the landing sites seem close together, even walkable. "Can you take us there?"

She shakes her head. "Fox Red is a long way down the beach and difficult to get to. I'm sorry, no." She's on a scheduled route of stops, she says, and if it were closer, maybe, but she has no choice, she says. I'm disappointed but not surprised. The area is packed with tourists like us, and she must follow the schedule and bring us back to the museum on time.

"I'll wait here," she says, cutting the engine. "Take your time."

The wind is strong. It's midafternoon, and rain threatens. At the bridge, Ellen and David read dedication plaques while Edwin walks parallel to the shoreline, and Bill heads toward the water. I linger at memorials, both official commemorative plaques and homemade tributes, many painted by school children, placed around the base of the walkway over the beach. "Merci" one says, accompanied by a drawing of a dove. "Pax" reads another, followed by a series of words I don't know.

I look below to see Edwin kneeling on the beach, scooping sand into an empty water bottle. "I don't think that's legal," I say when he climbs the steps to the bridge.

"Then don't tell anybody." He smiles.

I glance back at Sandrina, thinking she might instruct him to return it, but she is talking with another tour guide beside the van, her back to us.

Around Edwin's neck and tucked inside his shirt hangs the chain with our father's dog tags. The wind and cold are almost unbearable as they whip around my neck and face. I join Bill at the water, and together we head back to the walkway, looking down at the rough channel waves.

Sandrina has joined us at the memorial site and stands with us as we gaze toward the water of this hallowed beach. "Theirs was a day much like this one," she tells us as we walk back to the van. "Brisk winds. Rain. A hard day."

Back in the van, we circle around nearby houses, following a winding road, until we reach the Normandy American Cemetery, and again, Sandrina hangs back as we walk through rows and rows of solemn gravestones. The site is eighteen acres of hilly land, she tells us, filled with almost 9,500 graves marked by crosses and Stars of David placed side by side. So many lives, so many stories that ended that first day of the invasion and in the days that followed.

Later we stand at the top of Pointe du Hoc, where US Army Rangers scaled this steepest cliff along the Normandy shoreline and captured the German stronghold, and finally we drive to Juno, Gold, and Sword Beaches, assigned to Canadian and British forces. When Sandrina lets us off at the Caen Memorial Museum, the site itself is closed for the day, the parking lot empty of vehicles, save for our van and a sprinkling of tour vans and a few other cars.

"Good luck with your journey," she says, as we depart. "The French people owe so much to you, and we will not forget."

CHAPTER 8

In the days that followed my father's death, no one mentioned him except the widows who came to visit my mother in the afternoons. They would sit beside Mama on the couch in the living room, cup their hands over hers, and speak in soft voices that I couldn't hear and didn't want to. At school, not talking about him was easy because just being around me seemed to make everyone uncomfortable. I felt like something was wrong with me, a basketball-sized growth on my face or a hairy, dead thing trailing off my shoe, and no one dared to mention it, perhaps no one was brave enough. One day he was here and the next day he was not, and there was nothing else to say.

Or maybe I was the one who didn't want to talk, and I threw up a wall no one dared penetrate. Mrs. Craven, my algebra teacher, pulled me aside after class one day and said, "You can't keep everything bottled up inside." I assured her I was fine.

My friends went in together and bought me a pair of gerbils, complete with a glass tank for them to live in and a small wheel for running. I didn't know whose idea it was, but it was a good one because it became my distraction. I spent hours watching them race in their wheel going nowhere, their little bodies working hard. My friends and I could talk about the gerbils instead of my father, and if I ever felt alone I could pick one up and feel the tiny feet running all over me and remember I was alive.

I did not want to participate in all-state band that spring. I had tried out and been accepted back in the winter when everything was different, but I didn't have the words to refuse when that May weekend arrived. On a Friday afternoon after school seven band friends and I headed to the small town of Burlington, an hour's drive from home, which was hosting the event this year. I loved playing my bassoon, which I'd learned only a year earlier. Daddy had loved hearing me play it, said it made him think of fall. Now, its deep wood tones and mournful bass notes were sounds I wanted to make from some dark place inside me.

Each student was assigned to a host family who offered hospitality and transportation to practices over the three-day weekend. My host family included two children in addition to the daughter, who played flute in the band. On Friday night, after our initial practice, the son, a fifth-grader, bugged me so much to play Yahtzee that I finally gave in and let him win, so he'd be happy. The first-grade daughter took to me like I was her big sister, and she pressed next to me when we spread out on the floor to play games, almost scooting over into my lap. I didn't mind. I felt comfortable in that house and for the weekend, it was easy to pretend it was my own family, my own life. Saturday morning, the father drove us to practice, chatting about the band, the other students from Asheboro, and asking me about the bassoon. He had a full head of brown hair, was shorter than my father, and younger, and was a lawyer. After dropping us off, he headed to the golf course, promising he'd see us that evening and be at the concert on Sunday

All that Saturday, we practiced new music, trying to perfect it—after all, our director kept telling us, we were the best in the state, and we should be quick to master the most advanced pieces.

The first chair bassoonist who sat beside me was the son of a bassoon professor at a university, and the son didn't talk to me or even acknowledge my position beside him. The third chair bassoonist talked too much about nothing important, was consistently flat, and was always losing her place and whispering to me for help. At second chair, I was somewhere between those two, I supposed, in both personality and talent.

My host mother picked us up that afternoon. We'd have a quick dinner then return to the auditorium for a final practice. "I look forward to meeting your parents tomorrow," she said.

I didn't hesitate. "Just my mother is coming." Lying, which I'd begun to do a lot, was getting easy. "My father is in New York on a business trip."

"I'm so sorry," she said. "Does he go there often?"

"Yes, often." I knew my eyes were twitching, giving away my lie, so I turned away so she wouldn't see them. Already, only two months after his death, I'd learned that the best thing to do, even if it hurt me, was not tell the truth. If you did, you'd get that many more questions and that many more people saying, "I'm sorry," and then moving away from you so they wouldn't have to talk.

"Well, how interesting," she said, and I knew that was the end of our conversation.

Our Sunday concert was scheduled for early afternoon, so we practiced in the morning and for lunch ate sandwiches that the host parents had brought in. We had dressed that morning in our concert outfits—black skirts or slacks and white shirts—so we were ready at one o'clock with enough time after lunch to warm up with a few scales. I looked for my mother from the stage and saw her halfway back in the middle of the auditorium, her curly black hair rising above other heads.

After the concert, parents were to meet their children, gather suitcases, thank the hosts, and head home. By the time I came down the stage steps into the auditorium, Mama had already found my host family—all of them, little brother, little sister, mother in a yellow dress, father in his gray Sunday suit and tie. Just as I came within reach, I heard my host mother say, "I'm so sorry your husband couldn't come today."

I looked down at the floor, knowing how ashamed I'd be when my mother told her the truth. Instead, Mama kept her eyes on me for longer than necessary and said, "He would have really enjoyed it." I had done the right thing. I had not told our secret.

I grabbed my suitcase, and I said goodbye and thank-you to my hosts. As we slid into our station wagon, I saw my weekend family through the glass as they walked to their car. The boy was racing ahead, the mother talking with her daughter the flutist, the father, holding the hand of his other daughter, and the little girl was skip-walking, and I turned away.

That spring and summer, Edwin stayed at Clemson, visiting on occasional weekends or the short breaks between classes. Mama encouraged him to stay at school, to dig in and master his classwork. Her life, more than ours, I think now, had changed drastically, and I overheard phone calls and conversations with friends that offered snippets of the challenges she faced: she was holding down a full-time teaching job at the high school; finishing work on a degree in guidance and counseling so she could move out of the classroom and into an office to work one-on-one with students; paying all bills on one salary and planning for three college educations. Nightly, she'd sit on the couch, the box of bills and financial obligations balanced on her lap. She had a head for money, and she knew who to call when she needed help with plumbing or yardwork or other household expertise. She was sick a lot, respiratory stuff that would improve with antibiotics. "You don't eat enough," Mama Bunting would tell her. "Are you sleeping?" No, she wasn't. At night, awake myself, listening to all-night talk radio, I'd see her light on or hear her footsteps down the hall. Now and then, she would push open my door and say, "Turn it off, Barbara, and go to sleep."

If her financial and physical worries weren't enough to bear, her social groups began slipping away. The bridge club, dinner-group friends, church friends. If I knew this then, I had no sympathy. She had no time for emotion. What we children saw as mean and un-reasonable might have been her way of holding onto what strength she had, getting by the best she could. When Daddy was alive, she was hardworking and organized, but Daddy could get her laughing, or she'd sing to the radio in her high-pitched voice, or she'd be out in the yard throwing snowballs with us. Without Daddy, the circles under her eyes grew darker, she fell asleep on the couch with the bill box in her lap, she had long stretches of silence. Not one time did she shed tears, at least not around us. I had no sympathy, so caught up in my own sorrow.

At home Ellen and I stayed quiet, helped as we could, and did our best, without talking, even to each other, to find our way out of our old life and into our new. We had no instruction and no sup-port other than our mother's rules and example, we had no ideas for our own recovery or even the realization that we needed recovery. Ellen turned to friends, and I turned to my notebook and music, closing the door to my room after dinner, so I could be by myself. For the three of us, darkness shrouded our home, even if the world around us was moving forward into the light of summer.

One evening during dinner, Ellen began telling a lively, funny story about something that happened at school. She forgot where she was. She'd had a good day, and she was happy and had forgot-ten that she wasn't supposed to be happy. As she waved her fork like a baton, talking, Mama's eyes locked on the chicken breast on her own plate. She picked up her knife, cut a slice, poked it with her fork, and bit into it without looking at me or, it seems, listening to Ellen.

Ellen collected friends like the dolls she cherished as a child. She lined them up and looked at them often, relishing each one. My friends, the ones I had before, no longer felt like friends, or else I didn't know what a friend was anymore. Nobody knew what to say to me, so they didn't say anything. The friend I liked still was Ann, who was not popular, who made a bad slip one day in Latin class when we were talking about how we'd all get home from the end-of-year Roman banquet. Ann forgot and said, "Maybe Barbara's dad can pick us up." Ann lived around the corner from us on Worth Street, and Daddy often picked up neighborhood kids, including Ann, after an event. Everybody, including Mrs. Parsons, our teacher, gave her that look, like "how could you?" and Ann slid down in her seat trying to hide. I was the only one who didn't mind because Ann was the first person who had even mentioned my father in all those months, and it was like she still thought of him as alive. I loved her for that but never told her. Maybe a friend was someone who, like me, wouldn't let him go.

But Ellen was different. Everybody was her friend. She always said, "I like so-and-so. She's funny." To which I would always say, "Do you like people just because they're funny?"

And she'd always answer, "Well, it doesn't hurt."

Which was true.

On this day it was Debra, and I liked Debra too because she was funny, but she also didn't mind me being around. They had been in the cafeteria at lunch, Ellen was telling us, when somebody came up to somebody and said something and Debra said something in response. Ellen started laughing so hard remembering it that she couldn't get the punch line out. I started laughing not so much because Debra was funny but because Ellen's giggling had started me giggling, and soon our plates were rocking and the table was shaking, and we couldn't stop. The more she laughed, the more I laughed, and for the first time in months everything felt like it used to.

Mama put down her fork and took a deep breath. She looked at Ellen with eyes that could have burned a hole through her, and then she turned to me until I was scorched too, and she said, "There is nothing funny in this house."

We stopped cold, the air in the room suddenly frigid.

"I'm sorry, Mama," Ellen said, her head down.

The hands on the oven clock moved forward. A finch, settled on the feeder for a beak full of seeds, flew away. Under the table, I nudged Ellen's foot with mine as if to say, "I thought it was funny," and she glanced at me quickly as if to say, "I did, too."

We finished the rest of our dinner without talking, and Mama dipped a spoonful of vanilla ice cream in little dessert bowls for each of us. "Do you have much homework to do?" she asked, to make conversation.

Ellen said, "Not much." She was a junior, taking college prep classes, but her favorite class was home economics, where she got to try out new patterns and complicated stitches on machines with a lot of attachments. I often wore her best results.

"Why do you let your sister dress you?" my friend had asked, and my only answer was that I liked what she made me, which seemed reason enough.

"My homework's finished," I said. "Except some reading for Mrs. Lucas's class."

We were moving like snails now, Ellen and I clearing the table and loading the dishwasher while Mama wiped the stovetop around the electric burners, even though they didn't need it. As soon as the kitchen was spotless, we headed to Ellen's bedroom while Mama went to the den to read the paper.

We closed the door to her room and sat across from each other on the twin beds. I played my Sears guitar, and we sang "Blowin' in the Wind," "Five Hundred Miles," and "The Times They Are A-Changin'," old folk songs we'd sung years earlier at Girl Scout camp and still loved. We took turns doing the harmony, we thought we were good, I laughed when Ellen closed her eyes and got that dreamy look on her face when we sang "Scarlet Ribbon," holding the last note until we both spurted out our breath, laughing. We were so good, I said, we should form our own sister act, and Ellen smiled and said maybe. We kept our voices down so Mama wouldn't hear us.

That night after I went to my room and crawled under the covers, a tomcat wailed outside the window. I lay in bed and listened to his throaty merowls, and I swore I heard a cat in the basement merowling back. In the morning before school, Mama sent me down to open the basement door and free the cat who had somehow gotten stuck in that closed space. It felt like things from the outside were coming to get us, but sometimes it felt more like our enemy was what was inside.

One morning we woke up to find a snake coiled on the braided rug in the den. He'd come in with the logs we hauled from the carport to the fireplace the night before to take the chill out of the house. I got the shovel from the basement, and Ellen scooped him up and tossed him out into the woods behind the house. One night a flying squirrel swooped down the chimney while we slept. He circled my mother's head when she walked through the den to the kitchen the next morning. Her screams woke us. The three of us chased the squirrel all over the house until we finally trapped it in Edwin's bedroom, opened the window, and closed the door. When we got home that afternoon, he was gone.

My mother's dream house was not her dream anymore. We felt trapped, like the critters, but no one stood by with a shovel to scoop us out, and no one opened a window so we could fly.

We knew that every Sunday when we turned out of the church parking lot after eleven o'clock services, Mama would head left instead of right, and we'd drive through town and onto Park Street as though we were meeting someone for Sunday lunch.

But then she'd pass through the entrance to Oaklawn Cemetery, cross the first intersection, curve around to the right at the second, then drive a few feet, pull up onto the grass, out of the way of any passing cars or walkers, and cut the engine. Ellen carried the grass clippers. I held the whisk broom and the plastic bag of fresh silk flowers.

We did the drill without talking—opening the car doors, stepping out, climbing the slight hill, up past three, four, five gravestones until we reached the white marble marker with corner vases that said PRESNELL on one side, BUNTING on the other. Our father's was the only body here, on the right side closest to the road. The World War II commemorative brass plate, provided by the American Legion, marked the foot of the plot and detailed his service information. Faded flowers, once a bright pink, surrounded now by pale leaves, looked forgotten, though not from inattention. We were here last Sunday and the Sunday before and the Sunday before that, trimming grass and brushing away dirt. Once a month, Mama would say, "It's time to refresh the flowers," and we'd go by K-Mart on Saturday afternoon and pick through the selection of fake bouquets, matching our choice of colors to the season.

It didn't matter how hungry we were, that we'd left a roast cooking in the oven, or that we simply did not want to be here, which was true for me. I didn't know what Ellen thought because I didn't ask, and we didn't talk about this ritual just like we never talked about anything, but she never complained. Neither did I, of course. Once Ellen asked if she could go home instead. She had some homework or she was meeting a friend in the afternoon. But Mama shushed her. It was one of those things we just did; and I did it, and Ellen did it, week after week.

I hated the weekly ritual. It was enough to know when I woke up every morning that my father was gone, but this habitual visiting reminded me week after week of the harshness of that gone.

We didn't ask why. We'd been raised to do the right thing, whatever that meant to our mother. We kept up appearances, and even our final resting places had to be attractive and swept clean, as though death itself could look good and feel better with proper care. That's how I understood our ritual, and that's how I learned to hate doing the right thing.

"Looks like they mowed," Mama said. "Left some weeds around the head of your daddy's stone for you to clip, Ellen. And, Barbara, you need to sweep off the grass clippings." She busied herself with lifting last month's flowers from the vases and bending the plastic stems of the new ones until they sat at the right height to show off the best angles. We each worked silently and alone in our thoughts.

When I was finished, I sat on the grass, even though I was in a dress, and waited for Mama to be satisfied with her work, so we could get back in the car and go home.

"I think it looks good, don't you?" Mama said. She walked around to the back side where she studied the plots for her parents as though the bodies were already underground, then came to stand at Daddy's footstone. She never cried. Ellen and I never cried. We were robots, circling a grave. We ourselves were stones, doing what we had to do, not allowing ourselves to feel. What lived in me was a longing so deep I didn't even realize it was there.

CHAPTER 9

Edwin is driving, and I'm navigating, paper maps spread across my knees, trying to make my Google printouts match the van's navigational system screen. We turn onto the N13 highway heading east out of Bayeux, France, toward Utah Beach, and I look up to see the sign: OMAHA BEACHES, TURN HERE. The road we traveled yesterday, heading toward the shoreline where tourist buses unload, splits off to our left. Edwin glances over and, in a voice so soft only I can hear, asks, "Wanna try to find Fox Red?"

Sandrina suggested that this most extreme beachhead was a long way down the beach, but she was also on a prescribed tour route within a limited time period. Now is our chance to do this trip our way, to not let tour guides make decisions for us.

I glance to the back seat, where Bill, Ellen, and David are nodding off to sleep. If we wake them and ask, it seems likely that someone will object. Sometimes it's best not to ask. "Let's do it."

Edwin turns right and we rumble down the uneven road to the beach where we'd been yesterday. Once we reach the route running parallel to the shore, all we need to do is drive east until we run out of road, right? Surely, that will be Fox Red. Ours isn't a well-thought-out plan, especially in this country where posted street and highway names don't always agree with map directions. But following our instinct—when we both agree—makes perfect, if precarious sense.

And so, with the others in the back seat unaware of our change in plans, I make a pact with Edwin, riding shotgun as we head off on adventure. We are of the same mind for the first time in at least forty-five years. I look over, not lingering so he won't think I'm staring, but with a glance, turning him into that skinny nineteen-year-old boy whose life took a drastic turn when he was least able to navigate the challenges he suddenly faced.

Still, I believed in him back then. The summer after our father died, I sent him a birthday card with a tiger on the front that looked like the Clemson mascot he adored. I knew he'd love it. I knew he'd call and ask just for me. I waited by the phone when he talked with Mama, thinking she'd hand me the receiver any minute. She didn't. The following fall, I stitched two purple Clemson pillows with orange tiger paws, one for him and one for me. I packed his in a box and mailed it, but he never responded, never thanked me.

In the years that followed, Mama tried to make him disciplinarian, a job I suspect he didn't want and rarely one he acted on. She wrote him letters, "telling" on me: "I found cigarettes in Barbara's coat pocket." "I'm pretty sure Barbara's been drinking." I know this because she read the letters out loud to me. I begged her not to mail them, because I didn't want him to be mad at me. I don't know if she sent them or not. I never heard from him. He never asked how I was, never followed up on her complaints, at least not with me.

His promise to take care of me was one no nineteen-year-old should have made, especially on the day of his father's death, and one no fourteen-year-old should have believed. I don't think either of us knew that; I longed to be the center of his world like I felt I was the center of my father's. Not only was I not the center; my brother didn't think about me at all.

My junior year in high school, our relationship hit a low. It was a Saturday in spring, and Edwin had come home for the weekend.

Just before noon, a yellow Volkswagen bug pulled up to our curb, and my friend Silas got out and walked to the house. He was on his lunch break from Fox Drug where he worked making deliveries. He was in my study hall, where we shared a table and had become good friends.

I knew what my mother thought, feared, and as I was passing through the kitchen, she stopped me. "I don't mind your being friends with Silas," she said, "but you need to be careful. People will think you're dating."

"You don't like him because he's Black."

"I like Silas just fine. It's your reputation I'm concerned with. I know how people will talk, what they'll say."

What people? I wanted to ask. And whose reputation was she trying to preserve? She knew Silas from her classes at the high school, and I knew she liked him, but this wasn't about Silas himself. She'd grown up in a household with parents who valued what others thought, parents who also maintained the strong racial prejudices prevalent in their generation. She struggled with many of her parents' beliefs even as she worked to change them. We were years beyond the Civil Rights Act, but decades, if not generations, before resolution.

When Edwin heard the disturbance in the kitchen, he stepped in. "Do what Mama says," he told me. "And don't argue."

I didn't expect this scolding. If this was his idea of being man of the house, I wanted none of it.

"Why should I care what you think?" I asked. "You don't live here anymore."

He drew his hand back and swung it hard, hitting my cheek with a blistering slap. I raised my fist intending to hit him as hard as I could wherever I could land a punch, but he grabbed my wrist before I made contact.

Mama looked as shocked as I was. We didn't hit in our house, except as children scuffling in the yard, and then we were punished. Edwin and I used to wrestle in the living room, and sometimes he'd let me pin him, but most of the time, he held me down until I called "uncle." What just happened was not play-fighting. This was real. Nobody had ever hit me like that, and I vowed right then that no one ever would again.

I turned away from the kitchen, from my mother and my brother, and I climbed in the car with Silas and didn't look back. When I returned to the house, no one mentioned it then or ever again, and Silas never came back to the house, though we remained friends.

My brother graduated from college. He married and moved to Augusta, Georgia, where his new wife's parents lived. In the years that followed, he fathered two children, advanced in his career, came home to Asheboro occasionally but not often, called Mama every Sunday night, and forgot about me.

Day by day, year by year, we quit being brother and sister. He rarely spoke to me, and I rarely reached out to him. When he brought his family to visit for Christmases or occasional summer weekends, my mother insisted Ellen and I come home as well so we could all be together. He and I had little to say each other. That's how it was. I quit expecting anything from him. I grew to hate him. Then I learned not to care.

At the Omaha beachfront, already beginning to crowd with tourists unloading from vans, we pause at the intersection facing the water. "Go right?" Edwin asks, though he knows the answer.

"Go right," I respond. He turns onto Rue Bernard Anquetil which runs parallel to the ocean and eventually curves into Rue de la 2ème Division US, the ocean to our left and fewer and fewer houses to our right. When that road ends at a large rock wall and there is no way forward, he pulls the van to a stop beside the wall.

The sleepy back seaters begin to wake. "Are we at Utah Beach already?" asks Ellen.

"Surprise! This is Fox Red." My brother and I high-five, satisfied with ourselves.

Oddly, no markers greet us, just an open and empty beach. "You'd think there'd be a sign or something," Edwin says.

A rain mist envelops us. I spot what looks like an information station at the top of the hill above the beach. "That's probably it," I say.

I trek up the hill, Ellen close behind, expecting to confirm our find. Through the raindrops that blur the surface of the plexiglass case, I consider the map on the inside. A red **X** marks our current spot—the east end of Easy Red. We haven't even moved out of the middle segment of Omaha Beach.

But the map is clear: drive away from the beach to the next intersection then follow the road east and cut back toward the shoreline. That will be Fox Red.

"It looks like we're almost there," I say. "We might as well find it now, and then we'll head on to Utah. A short side trip is all."

Again, Edwin and I smile, ignoring the grumblings from the others, and at the same time we say, "Let's go."

The channel is north, Fox Red is east. That much we know. I take a picture of the encased map, and we use it to guide us as we drive inland, following the narrow, curvy, unlined French road away from the beach. At the first intersection, we turn back toward the water, down a narrowing seaside road where a few small houses are set back into the hillside. Down a steep hill, the road ends at the water. A small village with a grocery store, a pub, and a sandwich shop on the corner faces the water. A long dock harbors a row of old fishing boats and an occasional dinghy. Edwin parks in a diagonal spot curbside, and we walk to the water.

"I don't think this is it," I say.

"I don't see a marker," Ellen says.

"This has to be it," says Edwin. "We did exactly what the map said."

"Something tells me the map left off some steps," I say. "Do we keep going, or do we give up and head to Utah Beach?"

I'm not sure everyone was on board with the plan when they first realized what Edwin and I were up to, but the idea has now become a mission. "Let's give it one more try," Ellen says. No one objects.

We drive back up the hill to the road that runs parallel to the channel. At the next left turn, we trek through a neighborhood and follow a gravel then a dirt road to a private drive that ends with a large, toothy dog defending its yard.

Edwin backs up the van, does a quick Y-turn, and heads out of the neighborhood. Driving east again, he pauses at the next left intersection. As we debate turning or not turning, the van's tires sink into mud. All of us except Edwin step out while he rocks the vehicle back and forth until it pulls free.

We've been at this for a while now, and our early start has turned into a late-morning delay. Back in the van as it rumbles slowly down an unmarked highway, Ellen says, "I feel like we're on a wild goose chase. This was a good idea, but I think we've given it our best shot." We're farther and farther away from the shore, farther and farther from Omaha Beach, not to mention Utah.

David, who has kept quiet since waking up almost an hour ago, speaks up from the back seat. "Did anybody see that sign back there?"

"What sign?"

"I'm pretty sure it was a picture of a fox. It was in French, but it might mean something." Edwin cuts another Y-turn in the middle of the road and retraces our route. On the left, a small white sign with a red drawing and black letters is posted on the highway. "Le Renard Rouge," it reads. The cartoon red fox points to the words, "Chambres d'Hotes. Bedroom Zimmer. Gites."

"'Rouge' is red," Bill says, recalling his high school French. "I'm not sure about 'renard,' but that's definitely the picture of a fox. I'm not positive, but I think this is a bed-and-breakfast called Red Fox. It can't be a coincidence."

A man is standing at a mailbox by the roadside. Edwin pulls onto the shoulder, and I hop out.

"Excuse me sir," I say. "We're looking for Fox Red, the beachhead?" His English is only slightly better than my French. I ask several times, changing my words and making hand gestures until I see his eyes brighten in understanding.

"Oui, oui. Yes, go down that lane." He points to a road in front of the inn that leads to the water. "At the end, you will find your Fox Red."

The narrow lane he directs us onto ends at the waterfront. A long sidewalk stretches along the water, and a small grocery store/café peers down from the top of the hill, a parking lot below it.

We leave the van and hike up the hill to the store. The door is locked, but a man behind the counter sees us, heads over.

"You are close," he says in English. "Follow the sidewalk east till it runs out, then walk down the path. Maybe three, four hundred meters. You'll see the cliffs, a white house at the top of the hill. That's Fox Red."

Morning rain has slickened the wooden steps leading back down to the sidewalk. Bill and I lead, Edwin follows, and Ellen and David hurry behind. A few yards from the path, I hear a yelp and turn to see Ellen, sprawled on the sidewalk.

"Damn it," she says. "I don't need this." She lifts the cuff of her capris to see that there is no blood, but the knee is already beginning to swell. She tries to stand, but the slightest weight makes her groan.

"You'll have to go without me. I don't think I should try it," she says. She glances at David, who's kneeling beside her.

"You can hold onto me," I say. "We can all help."

"No." She's sitting now on the wet wood, her face wincing, her eyes tearing, with pain or frustration, I'm not sure. "Take lots of pictures."

When she's settled on a bench near the path, David beside her, we take off, single file, Edwin, me, and Bill, down the path. I look back at Ellen, who is watching us, holding her knee. I want to go back for her. I want to carry her. We've come this far, and it doesn't seem right to leave her behind. But Edwin races ahead. I jog to catch up, following his steps.

To our left, a pristine shoreline stretches along the beach of the blue-green channel water. To our right, yellow buttercups wash over a hillside that climbs higher and higher; the sand at our feet becomes small pebbles.

The white house we are looking for sits at the top of the hill. Rock and grassy cliffs, steep, with an occasional gulley cut by erosion provide the only passage up. The waves gently washing onto shore are hushed. This beach does not resemble Easy Red in any way except its serenity; the strand itself is narrower, the cliffs rising higher and flanked by rocks.

Casualties on Fox Green, adjacent to Fox Red, were among the highest recorded on June 6, the D-Day invasion. Fox Red, with fewer casualties, also saw intense counterattack by Germans, but the narrow beach and the high cliffs helped soldiers scramble to safety.

According to accounts by veterans, most of which appear on Frank Towers's website, on the day our father landed, June 12, the beach was quiet except for the moaning of wounded soldiers, sedated, lying on the sand, and waiting for transport to field hospitals. Parts of tanks, trucks, and other weaponry and equipment destroyed by bombing littered the beach. Over the cliff and through the hedgerows, intense fighting continued.

I picture our father, his pack heavy, ammunition belt strapped around his waist, his rifle high in the air, trudging through the ice-cold water of the English Channel then, as the water becomes more shallow, racing to the shoreline. I marvel at the steep rise of the rocks, imagine young soldiers scrambling. Bill follows a narrow path that leads up the steep incline, climbing on his hands and knees to the top. "Once they got up here," he calls down, "there's nothing but hedgerows."

Edwin and I stand side by side staring into the water in front of us, and we turn to face the cliff. When Edwin slides his arm around me and squeezes my shoulder, I turn for a full hug, perhaps the first time I have put my arms around him since our mother died fourteen years earlier, and the act was more obligatory than genuine. Now, my embrace is full of spontaneity and joy. His large arms don't hug lightly. He pulls me into his chest, and I rest my head against his shoulder, brushing away tears. Bill stands back, giving us this moment.

Edwin reaches for a chunk of driftwood and begins to write across the shoreline. I slip off my shoes despite the cold and dig my bare toes into sand. Using the heel of my shoe as a writing instrument, I join Edwin in scripting a message. In letters tall and wide enough to be seen by a plane passing overhead, we spell out,

"WGP," our father's initials, and "June 12, 1944," the day he ran up the beach where we now stand.

When we've photographed every rock and shrub of this place, we retrace our hike to the parking lot, and there, on a picnic table, is Ellen, her knee swollen to twice its normal size. She's watching down the beach for a sign of us, and, seeing us, she waves. David sits beside her, his hand lightly resting on hers.

By now, the midday sun has centered itself in the sky, and wind whips around my collar and blows my hair. I stand beside Edwin, looking out over the channel. We've done this thing, I think, together from the start. Something has shifted between the two of us. Maybe I could like him, I think. Maybe I could love him.

CHAPTER 10

The spring before my father died, he stopped one Friday on the way home from Lumberton at an alpaca sweater factory outlet and brought me a V-neck, button-up, dark blue sweater. Alpaca sweaters were the rage, and I had begged him for weeks to bring me one, just as when I was younger, I would beg him to bring me sweatshirts and T-shirts from the mill. But he'd forget and forget again or get too busy. Just as he forgot to pick me up from scouts or school, or he'd get so busy, the time would slip by, and there I'd be, standing on the curb with my friends, waiting. But he never let me down, he never didn't come. I'd see that white Corvair speeding up the road, headed our way. He'd slow to a stop, his windows down, and holler out, "Y'all need a ride?" and we'd pile in the car like he wasn't late, and he'd drop us off one by one. The sweater, when he finally handed it to me on that wintry Friday afternoon, was perfect—a loose weave, sleeves just long enough that I could cuff them, an indigo blue that I thought highlighted the brown of my eyes. I wore it all that weekend and every day the next week until Mama made me take it off so she could clean it.

After he died, the sweater remained on a hanger, never worn. I'd sneaked his green Saturday work shirt from his closet along with a striped tie. I pushed the three of them together in the far corner of my closet and if anyone else knew they were there, they didn't say. I could keep secrets, and secrets became more and more important. I could immerse myself in memories, I just couldn't share them or say them out loud.

In the summer before my junior year of high school, Rebecca moved into our neighborhood and became the only person in my life who had not known my father. I was learning not to talk about him, and to do as my mother insisted, I couldn't tell Rebecca even if I wanted to, but I didn't want to because I liked not being the girl whose father died, which is how I felt around everyone else. I didn't want her to treat me differently, the way it seemed everyone else did.

Rebecca was smart, confident, and angry that her father's new job forced her to leave her hometown of High Point for her last two years of high school. She never pretended to like her new home; she simply tolerated it. What she loved was the life she left behind, and maybe that's why I liked her. We both wanted what we didn't have. She lived two blocks from us on Cliff Road, and her father erected a basketball goal in her driveway. I often walked down, and we shot hoops on boring Saturdays or sat in her room playing records after school.

One October afternoon, her father picked us up at school after a late-afternoon math club meeting. It was a clear, cool fall day, colors swirling around us, leaves released from trees. "Jacket weather," my father used to call it, the season we would rake leaves, pile them high at the edge of the yard, and burn them until they sizzled cold after dark. His favorite season and mine too. Now, Mama had hired a yard man, and his crew took care of the leaves.

Rebecca was chatting with her dad in the front seat, laughing about something I couldn't hear. We were only a block from my house when she turned around to the back seat where I was sitting and said, "I sure hope your father's got better jokes than mine."

I froze. I didn't know what to say, so I didn't say anything except, "Thanks for the ride," when her dad pulled into my driveway and let me out. I closed the car door, headed straight for my bedroom, and worked on math assignments until Mama called me to help with dinner.

The next morning, when I arrived at school, Rebecca was waiting for me outside the auditorium before our morning assembly. We didn't share the same homeroom and didn't sit together during assemblies. She'd gone out of her way to find me.

"Hey!" she called. I saw her coming but acted like I didn't and instead turned the opposite way toward the front of the auditorium where my homeroom was gathering and away from Rebecca. I didn't want to see her, not now, not ever again. I was ready to end this friendship, which had suddenly become too hard.

She pulled my sleeve, said again, "Hey."

I turned, acted like I was seeing her for the first time. "Hey back."

"Just wanted to say, I'm sorry about yesterday."

"What?" As though I didn't know. Maybe we could gloss over this, I thought. Maybe I could.

"You should have told me your father died. My dad told me last night."

"It never came up." I shifted my books from one arm to the other.

"I feel really bad. It was stupid of me."

"It doesn't matter."

"Yes, it does. I should have known."

She had no idea that he used to drive me to school and pick me up, that he loved to fish and grow azaleas and take me along with him on errands, wherever he was going.

"Do you want to tell me about him sometime?"

I didn't. I couldn't. "I've got to find my seat for assembly, or I'll be counted tardy," I said, taking off down the aisle almost in a run to get away from her. I slid into the cold metal seat with all those old friends who knew, which seemed oddly comfortable, because I wouldn't have to tell them. I wouldn't have to say a word; I could just go on as I'd been doing, day by day, slipping into my silences. The microphone on stage crackled as a teacher began to speak. It was freezing in there. I thought about my blue sweater, tucked deep in my closet, but the thought could not keep me warm. All I had were books, which I hugged to my chest. I glanced back to where Rebecca was still standing, by the door, watching me, confused. I knew she would not let this go, but regardless of how much I wanted her friendship, I could not tell her anything.

CHAPTER 11

A few minutes before eleven o'clock, a tall, thin gentleman with thick, white hair and dark-rimmed glasses pushes open the door of the Hotel de la Poste in Mortain, France. A knit scarf is tucked around the collar of his blue jacket.

"Welcome to our town," Noël Sarrazin says and grips my hand with his, a strong handshake. He's the president of the 30th Infantry Division Association in Mortain, he tells us. "I am going to host you today. I am always honored when an American soldier or the family visits Mortain."

Noël wastes no time with small talk. "The 30th Infantry is my passion. I can tell you more and show you the town, but for now, we must hurry. The mayor is expecting us in a few minutes. I'm sorry," he says. "I am a little late getting here. My dog, you understand."

He motions to a truck parked on the curb, and there, at the window, is the face of a young border collie, gazing longingly at her owner. "Heidi," he says. "She's just a pup."

I smile. "I have one too." I don't know why Heidi is getting the blame for his tardiness, but I do know that dogs keep their own schedules, and my own has made me late many times.

The five of us, Ellen and David in the rear, fall in line and follow Noël down the sidewalk, cutting across the street, through an alley toward city hall. Morning air is blustery, and a gray sky threatens rain. I rush to keep pace with our guide up a steep avenue, and Ellen drops further behind.

"We have had a change of mayor recently," he says, when I note that the person we are meeting this morning is not who was originally scheduled. "Unfortunately, our mayor for a long time was diagnosed with cancer. It progressed quickly, and soon we found ourselves without. Our new mayor was serving as deputy mayor, and he was elected to stay on. It has been a difficult time, but I believe we are now in good hands."

I nod to acknowledge the loss. "We are grateful for the reception," I say. "It's a wonderful welcome."

"We French owe everything to the Americans. You will find everyone here is glad to see you. If not for the Americans, we would have remained under German occupation for much longer. American soldiers liberated our town," Noël says. "All of our towns."

When we pulled into Mortain at dusk last night, we were welcomed by a main street lined with French, British, and American flags. Even the hotel clerk seemed glad to see us.

Edwin catches up with Noël, Bill, and me. "Do you know the American Civil War? Mortain is the Gettysburg of World War II, would you agree?" he asks.

I've followed Bill to almost every Civil War battlefield in the South. While I don't understand the strategies of that war any more than this one, I do know that Gettysburg was a devastating defeat for the South and many, many lives on both sides were lost. The story of Mortain is similar, its Allied victory sending a loud signal to Hitler that his power was beginning to shift.

"It was a turning point," Edwin continues, "like Gettysburg."

"Yes, it's true," Noël says. "It ended domination by the Germans. We could envision victory over Hitler for the first time. Things might have ended differently if not for the Americans."

We reach the beige, multistoried building, enter through the glass doors, and board the elevator to the second floor where Sonia, the mayor's administrative secretary and my contact since my initial email, stands ready to greet us when the doors open. I walk toward her like an old friend—our emails have been numerous and cheerful. She greets me warmly, but, like Noël, she doesn't pause for small talk; instead she leads us to the mayor's office.

The man sitting in front of the window stands and walks around a surprisingly uncluttered desk to shake our hands. His name is Hervé Desserouer, but when he introduces himself, what I hear is "Silverware," which I scribble in my notebook to help me with pronunciation. He has thin, white hair, and his open-collared shirt is stretched tight over a Santa Claus-like belly. Unlike Noël and Sonia, he's relaxed, and for the first time, I can catch my breath. He shakes our hands, smiles, turns to Noël, and says something in French.

"Our mayor does not speak English, but he tells me that he is looking forward to getting to know you," Noël says. "He will join us shortly in the reception room where champagne and biscuits are waiting."

We follow Sonia and Noël into a ballroom bordered on three sides with large picture windows overlooking Mortain. Multitiered chandeliers add elegance to the otherwise ordinary room. An older man in a blue windbreaker waits by himself and acknowledges our arrival with a quick smile.

"Charles Lebrun," Noël says, and Mr. Lebrun bows slightly and reaches for my hand. He's dressed neatly in khaki from shirt and jacket to shoes. He stands as straight as a redwood, his large hands clasped in front of him.

Trays of cookies and cakes and a bottle of unopened champagne are arranged around the table. Mr. Silverware arrives with another gentleman who Noël explains is deputy mayor Jean-Paul Briend. He's small in stature and in build, and his face twinkles with a constant smile. I hear Noël call Briend the "petite mayor," which I write down in my notebook, though I'm not sure if it's a formal title or a descriptive term. The little French I know is so grossly Americanized that it doesn't help.

"Welcome, Americans!" Briend says and reaches to pop the cork on the champagne bottle. Foam spills over onto the floor. We laugh. It's early for champagne, for us Americans, at least, but we wouldn't dare refuse.

"To the people of Mortain!" says Edwin, holding his glass for a toast.

"Santé!" says the petite mayor. "To you!"

We smile and touch glasses, unsure what else to do. Of our hosts, only Noël speaks English. David, Bill, and Briend form a loose circle around him.

Ellen and I step toward Charles LeBrun and attempt a conversation. Whether he understands our questions or not, he responds in French, and I catch a "oui," which tells me either that something we said was correct or he didn't understand a word. Finally, he shrugs, shakes his head, and says, "My English is very bad."

"But it's much better than my French," I respond.

I glance at Edwin, who is standing beside the champagne table, talking with the mayor. One of Edwin's arms crosses his chest and is tucked under his elbow, and the other is lifted to his face, his hand cupping his chin—a familiar, pondering pose. His expression tells me he's working hard to make sense of the mayor's words. I overhear "development" and "business," and I imagine him in conversation about the state of the economy in Mortain, though I note a good bit of eye crinkling and head cocking by the mayor. I wonder if it's a one-sided conversation, though I'm not sure which side controls it. Edwin sees me, grins, and winks.

How I wish our father, who would turn ninety-eight this year had he lived, could be standing here with us, talking in awkward French to those he liberated. How he would love to share stories with Noël.

Almost an hour passes before Noël announces, "The mayor must leave to go to another meeting. If you would like, I can show you around Mortain, take you to the hill where the battle took place, and see the location of your father's unit."

A gentle rain has begun, glazing the stone buildings of Mortain when we step outside. Noël points to a small brasserie a few stops from Hotel de la Poste called "Café Sanwich."

"Are you hungry for lunch? It's good," he says. "And very popular. As you see, we don't have many restaurants in Mortain, but this I believe you will like."

I'm not at all hungry. Slightly tipsy from two glasses of champagne before noon, I'm more sleepy than hungry. The opportunity to sit awhile appeals.

Café Sanwich looks like an American sports bar. Television screens flash in corners. A patron's choice of liquors, wines, and beers, both on tap and in bottles, line shelves behind the bar. Logos, chalk menus, even samples of T-shirts for sale hanging on the wall behind the long wooden bar remind us of home. The server delivers a breadbasket, and jots down our orders of paninis, salads, and more bread.

Soon we learn that Noël is a good conversationalist. He has been interested in the war since he was a boy, he tells us, and as an adult he has worked hard to commemorate the American soldiers in the 30th Infantry Division and teach others about the battle. He doesn't elaborate when Ellen asks about his family. "Heidi," he says with a smile, "is my girl."

"I just want to ask one thing that's been on my mind," Edwin says during a pause. "Everyone has been so nice. How do the French really feel about us? I mean, France and the United States haven't always had the best relationship, especially in recent years."

Noël doesn't hesitate. "Every Norman is half American. It goes deep with us."

Ellen looks up from her plate. "You mean in their hearts?" We all know the stories of American GIs and their attraction to French women. It's a good question, but I want to hold my chuckle until I hear Noël's response.

"Yes," says our guide, a shy grin spreading across his face. "I'm sure there is American blood here. But we are so appreciative of what America did for us. We are all half American in our hearts." Noël takes a bite from his sandwich, and, still grinning, shifts his gaze to the screen playing across the back of the bar.

"It's true that the past has shaped who we are, and we cannot forget it," he continues. "Not only in our architecture and our rebuilding since that time, not only our losses, but in so many ways—and, yes, there are children—that war changed us."

War must have changed my father, too. What happened to him here we will never know. How this war shaped him, directed him, educated him must have made a difference, as it did to every soldier, for the good or the bad. This young millworker with a high school education joined the National Guard when he had no idea what he was signing up for. Five years and so much life experience later, he returned to the mill. But the man who returned was not the boy who left. He'd been a leader, a sergeant with a company of men depending on him. He'd seen life outside the little county of his birth, witnessed the deaths of close friends, and survived his own near death. Soon he'd have a wife, a family, and he would never stop talking about the war. Like our French guide, perhaps it meant everything, but what and how I would likely never know.

After lunch, we follow Noël's truck to the parking lot of La Petite Chapelle Saint-Michel, a stone chapel on a hilltop overlooking Mortain. Heidi rides with her head leaning out the window, throwing herself into the wind. She is the first of us out, and, as though she has been here many times, she races to the grassy yard and stops by a stone memorial to the 30th Infantry Division several feet from our vehicles. The red-and-blue Old Hickory emblem emblazons its center. Heidi scampers through the grass, circling the plaque, which reads, in English, "In homage of pious gratitude." Noël stands to the side and describes the ceremony, held only a year ago, when the memorial was dedicated.

"Everyone in town was present," he says. "We had representatives from all countries, and even some American veterans joined us. It was a glorious day." He pulls a notebook from the satchel he carries and shows us photographs and a newspaper account of the occasion. "Of course, as you can see, I am presiding." His pride is apparent in his bright eyes and the care with which he turns the pages of his book. "I don't have a connection to the war," he explains. "But it is a story I have known all my life. A story of our town. You have many enthusiasts in this country, many friends."

As Edwin, Bill, and I follow him up the asphalt trail beyond the monument, he continues, "Hill 314 is just above the chapel and across the road. Mr. Lebrun will meet us there." A light rain has begun to fall. Ellen, not trusting her knee on the wet ground, waits with David in the van. At the top of the road, Charles Lebrun steps out from a car and joins us at the edge of the woods. Here, beneath his black umbrella, he seems larger than he did this morning and perhaps he stands taller.

I already knew the basics of the story Mortain from books and Frank Towers's 30th Infantry Division website. In August 1944, two months after the invasion at Omaha Beach and four years after German occupation had begun, American forces arrived in Mortain to continue to push the Germans out of France and ultimately across the Rhine River. They liberated towns throughout Normandy as they marched south, but Mortain was a German stronghold. The first American attack was successful, but Hitler's troops regained control. Over seven hundred soldiers from our father's division were trapped by Germans at the edge of town on a hill called 314. For eight days, the men were without food, water, or ammunition until reinforcements arrived.

"Mr. Lebrun bought this land to preserve the story. This Hill 314." Noël reaches both hands out to greet Mr. Lebrun then turns back to us as the older man begins to talk.

"He was seventeen in 1944 and a young teen when Hitler's troops arrived and seized Mortain," Noël translates as Mr. Lebrun tells the story. "He lived through four years of German occupation and, like most French citizens, did not like being subject to German rule. At sixteen, a local barber hired him as an assistant and apprentice. He remembers one afternoon when he accidentally snipped the throat of a German soldier. He was almost shot until he convinced his occupiers that the slip of the razor was accidental."

"But was this accident?" Mr. Lebrun says in English and smiles.

When Germans returned to Mortain after the American's first attack, Noël continues, Mr. Lebrun's family fled in one direction to safety, and Charles, the oldest son, headed in the opposite direction—into the woods where he hid for those eight days.

"During that time, he risked his life to sneak food and water from a nearby farm up the hill to the trapped soldiers," Noël says. "Many French people did all they could to help the Americans and regain their freedom."

Mr. Lebrun is the first person we've met who was alive during the war, and he remembers details vividly, even though he is now eighty-seven years old. I walk beside him as we head to the top of the hill, so I can hear his voice, even though I can't understand his words. Noël walks a few steps ahead and listens closely, occasionally glancing over his shoulder to catch a phrase or explain to us.

Rain is steady now and early afternoon May temperatures are biting. We stand beneath an umbrella of oaks and birches, but rain finds us anyway, dripping from our heads and shoulders onto our pants legs. I'm still wearing sandals, my feet tucked into socks I slid on after the morning reception, and I fight my body's shivering.

"This sunken area is a foxhole," Noël says, pointing down into a grass-filled crater the size of a small backyard swimming pool. "It was dug by Germans when they occupied the hill, but Americans used it too." At the apex of the hill, a clearing between trees opens to two large granite rocks. Noël stands close to the edge and looks down at the landscape surrounding Mortain, "You can see why this was such an important spot for Germany."

He points to another small foxhole amid the trees. "Mr. Lebrun knew the American radio operator who set up in this spot," Noël continues. He doesn't explain how young Charles came to know the American soldier, but I imagine a friendship born of mutual contempt for the captors and a desire for freedom must have grown between them. Perhaps the American even came to his shop for a haircut in the days before the German counterattack.

A few steps further down the hill is the well where the men drew water, tucked against rocks that once concealed German soldiers lying in wait to capture them.

"But the well was not sufficient," Noël says "Lebrun and others carried water to the trapped soldiers. Americans attempted to drop supplies, but the drop missed the target, and the supplies were seized by Germans."

Charles Lebrun's khaki jacket repels the rain, and although his crooked blue umbrella is missing spokes, only a few drops wet his shoulders. Tucked under his arm is a plastic sheath and inside it a manila folder from which he lifts a faded aerial photograph of Mortain and hands it to me.

"He wants you to keep it," Noël says. I acknowledge Mr. Lebrun's gift with a smile and my Southern American version of "Merci," and then reach in my own folder and find for him the photograph of my father standing on the edge of the Elbe River.

"Merci," he responds, studying the photograph and nodding as Noël relays the story of the photograph as I have told it to him. I recognize the word, "pére," for father and "Elbe." Mr. Lebrun nods his head and bows slightly before slipping the photo into his folder.

Soldiers from my father's regiment orchestrated the rescue of the men trapped on Hill 314, attacking at dawn on August 12, 1944. Casualties at the end of the eight days were severe: of the seven hundred soldiers trapped, more than four hundred were killed, wounded, or captured. According to our father's journal, the Germans, feeling the pressure of Allied forces, fled Mortain and began to retreat from the region, signaling the end of the Battle of Normandy. One hundred days had passed since the D-Day landing. More than two hundred thousand Allied soldiers, and even more Germans, had lost their lives. It had been a devastating summer for both sides.

Noël interrupts my thinking. "Mr. Lebrun needs to get out of the weather." Charles Lebrun is perhaps the closest we've come to our father's time here, and he's exactly the kind of person I hoped to meet, one who could give a personal not just an historical accounting. I don't want to say goodbye, but Bill and I thank him, shaking his hand, and then walk back toward the parking lot where Ellen and David wait in the van. Noël follows us, and when he opens the door to his truck, a wet Heidi hops in.

Edwin hangs back, taking a last look at the site and lingering for the last words with our guide. After we climb into the van to get out of the rain, he hurries down the hill and slides into the driver's seat.

"The most remarkable thing just happened." He pauses to catch his breath. "I was telling Mr. Lebrun goodbye, and I shook his hand, and I told him how meaningful this day had been to me."

Mr. Lebrun, with strength Edwin didn't think he would have, gripped my brother's hands and held on. "Thank you, Americans," he said.

"Tears were pouring down his face," Edwin says. "We're only the children and he's so appreciative. What Daddy did, what they all did, it meant everything."

Mortain is surrounded by hills, and even the town, which sits in a valley, has its share of steep inclines. We pull out behind Noël and follow his truck. Occasionally, Noël stops on the shoulder of a road, hops out, and walks back to our van to point out a site or a structure of some importance. Finally, we pull over at the edge of a remote patch of land to the east of town. In front of us is a cow pasture. On both sides are thick growths of trees. Ahead, we again can see the village of Mortain and a clear view of Hill 314.

"Here, they were keeping lookout, monitoring the hill and the ground," Noël tells us. "The entire area was thick with German soldiers. Your father most likely was right here in this spot. He would have seen a good bit of war." To our left, hedgerows still separate fields, cutouts of tank-size holes still visible, just as they were seventy years before. Noël toes his boot into the edge of the asphalt, and a loose rock tumbles into the shallow ditch. I imagine my father standing beside this field, gazing out toward the hedgerows.

From here, we can see a shadow of the overhanging rock on Hill 314 where Noël stood a few hours ago to show us the town of Mortain. In front of us, cattle graze peacefully in a lush field. A white farmhouse sits behind us, a dense hedgerow lining the property.

"The hedgerows are so thick the Nazis used to hide tanks in them," Noël tells us. They were designed by French farmers to delineate borders and control water, wind, and soil, but not being used to them, American soldiers had great difficulty adjusting to them as weapons of war. "Just imagine how many German soldiers could duck into those tangled limbs and not be seen. Not only were they barriers against the enemy, but they were also dangerous places, because they could hide so much. The Americans dug their way through hedges many times, and many lives were lost."

Heidi hops out of the passenger seat of the truck and sniffs along the side. Few cars travel this remote passage. Noël allows us plenty of time to look. I walk out into the field by myself, imagining how it was seventy years earlier.

"Your father very likely saw this exact view," says Noël, coming up beside me. "They were posted here, at the edge of this field, ready to go in when needed."

I feel our father close, as though I'm breathing the air he breathed, as though it has circulated here all these years. Edwin joins us, his sleeve touching mine. Bill jots notes on a scrap of paper as Noël talks. Ellen and David look out over the tall grasses, their arms linked.

We follow Noël in his truck to one of his favorite natural sites, the Mortain waterfalls. "There is no significance to the battle here," he says, "but it is one of our most visited sites, and I believe it is the perfect place to end our day."

He's right. The Grand Cascade, as it is called, combines waterfalls formed by the Cance and the Cançon, two streams that spill down this mountainside, a rollicking wash of blue and white. With Heidi as our guide, we climb down the narrow path toward the water for a close view, the cool spray further dampening our faces and clothes. We're still wearing outfits from the morning reception. Edwin, in his suit coat and good shoes, hesitates before he too steps down the dirt path to the falls.

Afterward, we stand in the road, our vehicles parked on the edge, chatting, until the sun drops below the tree line.

"Maybe you will come back and visit us," Noël says and promises that he will tell us when he comes to America.

It's an awkward goodbye, as though neither of us wants the other to leave, as though we've connected as more than just friends, and I wonder if, in our hearts, perhaps we Americans are also half Norman.

CHAPTER 12

After Ellen left for college, it was just Mama and me in the many-roomed, hollow ranch house on Ridgecrest Road. We sat side by side for breakfast and supper, sometimes without a word shared between us beyond what it took to get food on the table and dishes off it. After dinner I retreated to my room and closed the door to finish homework, write in my journal, or play records. She fell asleep on the couch reading the paper or paying bills, woke up and came to my bedroom after my light was out, pushing my door open and tiptoeing in.

I knew she was there. She would tug my curtains together if any light shined through, and she closed dresser drawers and closet doors if I'd left them open, which I did almost every night. "Spirits will come out of them at night," she'd told me since I was a child. Now I knew she'd been right all along. Spirits of restlessness, loneliness, darkness, and confusion swirled around in my room at all times of day and night.

On the Friday of my eighteenth-birthday weekend that April, I packed my sleeping bag, laced on hiking boots, and headed with a small group of friends to a nearby Girl Scout camp. We spent Saturday canoeing Brownie scouts around the lake, teaching the little girls to make lanyards from strips of plastic, and waiting for dark when they boarded their bus and headed back to town. My friend Rebecca had sneaked a six-pack of beer from her father's refrigerator. It was warm from being hidden in her backpack all day; still, sitting by the campfire that night, we drank it all, and my friends sang, "Happy Birthday," a boisterous round that echoed through the trees. It was a perfect spring day and night and exactly what I wanted for my birthday.

That Sunday afternoon, we drove back to town, and Rebecca let me off at my driveway. My mother met me at the door, smiling too happily like something was up, but she simply said, "Go shower. You'll feel better when you get clean."

I didn't tell her that I felt just fine, finer than if I'd spent the weekend at home. But my mood was too good to spoil. I dropped my boots by the door, slid out of dirty jeans, and took a long shower, letting the water wash over my head, my shoulders, soap bubbling down my legs and swirling the drain.

Refreshed, I pulled on a clean pair of jeans, found a sweater in my drawer, picked out socks, and then reached into my closet for the moccasins I wore every day, but they weren't there, weren't anywhere.

My moccasins were gone.

Fringed around the edges, light tan, one single rawhide tie at the ankle. I loved them as much as I loved anything. They hadn't cost much at the Big Deal Shoe Store, and I wore them everywhere—to school, at home, out with my friends, walking with friends—everywhere, that is, except camping when I traded them for hiking boots and gave the moccasins a rest.

"Those things are filthy," my mother complained almost daily. "You can't clean them. And they have no support for your feet."

Everybody wore them, those of us in our bell-bottoms who hung around the back steps of the school, drama kids, band kids, smart kids, even athletes wore them. They were popular and comfortable, but to me, they were more than that. They were a style that nobody picked for me but me. Ellen hadn't made them, nobody had handed them down, I had bought them with my own money earned from babysitting neighborhood kids. In my moccasins, I felt most like me.

I stormed to the kitchen, fearing the worst. "Yes, I got rid of them," she said. "It was time for them to go." I headed out to the carport to dig through the garbage can, and she followed, saying, "No need to look. Garbage truck took them already."

When she realized I wasn't taking this well, she began a new plan. "We'll get you another pair. I'll go with you on Monday."

I felt so angry, so betrayed. I knew if I didn't go inside, I'd hit something, like the door or the car, or I'd grab her delicate arm and hurt it, but in the end, I'd be the one who got hurt.

It was almost dark. I spun around and turned away from her just as a brown-paneled station wagon turned into the driveway, slowed, then wound down the curved concrete and came to a stop. It was Rebecca. From the other side of the street, a light blue Volkswagen bug appeared. Paula. I glanced at Mama then back to the street as more cars pulled in, friends stepped out.

"Surprise," Mama said flatly, her voice attempting a rise. "I invited some friends over for a little party for your birthday. I thought you'd like that."

I didn't know how to feel. I hated her. I was so glad to see my friends. I wanted to tell them how terrible she was, how terrible my life was.

She'd made a caramel cake, my favorite. She was smiling, greeting my friends, most of whom she didn't like—at least I never thought so. I followed them in, my sock feet shuffling, and the cake, even though I didn't want it to be, was really good.

I needed to get out. I'd be going to college in the fall, but I didn't think I could make it another month, let alone two or three. I knew what I'd spend the summer doing: deep cleaning the house. It was what we did every summer, room by room, emptying cabinets and closets, scrubbing walls, washing windows. At least Ellen would be home on summer break from college, and together we'd find ways to make it not so terrible, like spraying each other with the hose when we headed outside to wash windows or sneaking to the den to watch TV when Mama answered a phone call that meant she'd be talking for a while. But it was terrible. Removing every single item from a closet so we could dust the shelves and wipe them clean with a rag dipped into a bucket of Spic and Span. Scrubbing walls, taking heating vents apart, rubbing beeswax on the furniture. Each room took the better part of a week, broken into tasks—one day the closets and shelves, one day walls and baseboards, and so on. We only took breaks when somebody gave us a bushel of green beans to preserve, or another chore broke into our house cleaning.

When in May the opportunity came for me to work that summer as a counselor at a church camp near Chapel Hill, appropriately called New Hope, I begged and pleaded until Mama said yes. I knew nothing about it. I got on the mailing list and received the brochure, because I sometimes visited the Presbyterian youth fellowship group that my friends attended. The prospect of the job excited me like nothing in a long time had. It meant getting away.

I left home in early June. At Camp New Hope, I spent my days teaching nine- and ten-year-olds to lash ropes, tie-dye T-shirts, make fires and tell stories around them. I made a slew of new friends who didn't know my story. It was a ten-week summer program, and I wouldn't go home until the week before I headed off to college. It felt like paradise. It felt like escape.

One day in mid-July, I received a letter during mail call in the dining hall after lunch. While the campers and other counselors sang camp songs before heading back to their cabins for a rest period, I sneaked out to the field just beyond the dining hall and dropped cross-legged to the grass. I'd lifted out the pages and skimmed the words when the camp nurse, Oma Lee, eased down on the grass beside me.

"Bad news?" she asked. Raising three children on her own might have aged Oma Lee prematurely, but it also helped her to parent many of us.

"My mother wants me to come home for the weekend," I said.

"There's a reason you don't want to go, isn't there?" she asked, reaching for my arm, a soothing mother's touch. I hadn't told her anything about me, but I felt like she knew. The letter, unfolded in my other hand, dropped to the ground. "She misses you."

If she missed me, I thought, it was because I was not home to help with summer cleaning. I pictured Ellen by herself with the scrub rag in her hand, wiping down walls, Mama sitting on her dressing table stool, ready to start vacuuming. Ellen was the one who should be asking for me. I felt bad that I left my sister alone, but I was here with new friends like Oma Lee, John, Mary, Jean. For the first time in years, I was away from my terrible life, away from my mother.

But to say that out loud about her felt like betrayal, so I tucked it in, just as I would tuck the letter beneath the T-shirts in my cabin's dresser drawer and not take it out until I threw it away at the end of camp.

"Don't be too hard on her," Oma Lee said. "She's trying."

I folded the letter, returned it to its envelope, and stuffed it into my pocket. Oma Lee and I sat together quietly until children began spilling from the dining hall, and my own campers came racing down the hill toward me.

When I did go home in mid-August, a week before I packed up and headed to college, I was storing summer gear on my closet shelves when my hand touched the journal, the one I'd left behind when I went to camp, a ring-binder with loose paper and narrow lines which I'd hidden on the top shelf of my closet before leaving for the summer. I was an occasional journal writer in those days, spewing venomous words in anger, hate, or frustration, usually at moments of high emotional intensity. Mama was the topic of many pages.

I flipped through, rereading my own words. When I turned to the last page, there was a familiar handwriting that wasn't my own, in black not blue ink, words written along the bottom lines.

"Just remember I love you," my mother had written. Her handwriting was precise, cursive, neat and attractive. She'd signed it, "Mom." I pictured her sitting on the edge of my bed, dust rag draped over one shoulder, my journal spread across her knees. I was furious, caught, violated, naked.

My anger spewed, as if a tight rubber band was rolling up my face and over my head. She'd read my words, my private thoughts, without asking, without telling. She'd stolen what was mine, and the least she could have done was not tell, pretend she hadn't read it, let me go on thinking my thoughts were private things and my bedroom was my own. Her "I love you" landed with a thud on the floor. I never mentioned to her what I'd found on that final page.

We live in our own sadnesses, building walls to shield us from others' pain when our own is all we can bear. It wasn't until years later, after Ellen told me a story about the summer when I was at Camp New Hope, when she was home alone with Mama, cleaning house, as though, with a rag and enough elbow grease, they could rid their lives of the accumulated grief.

I'd moved back from Kentucky to North Carolina by then, Mama had died a few years earlier, and Ellen lived less than an hour away. She had come to my house for the day to help me clean my kitchen. As adults we knew how to clean, and we joked about the irony of our work, that what we once spent three months doing, we now accomplished in one day. We'd take a day later in the summer and do the same kind of cleaning in Ellen's kitchen.

We'd washed shelves, reorganized recipes, and now we were hauling expired cans and boxes of food to the trash. Bird food, dog food, and people food covered kitchen counters and the breakfast-room table while we wiped the shelves clean and vacuumed from floor to ceiling.

"Mama and I were cleaning the house that summer," Ellen began. "And she says to me, out of the blue—" Ellen looked behind my shoulder instead of at me, after all these years still not comfortable with saying it out loud "—'it's my plan to kill myself after Barbara finishes school.'"

Ellen paused to let it sink in and then continued, "She kept a straight face. She didn't look at me. It was as if she'd been wanting to tell me but couldn't find the right moment. I think because she told me then, during our cleaning, was her way of saying there was no right time."

I was surprised, even jolted, by Ellen's story. I knew Mama was unhappy, but I didn't know or think she was capable of such thoughts. I didn't understand why she burdened Ellen and presumably no one else with her thoughts.

Ellen ducked into the pantry, lifted the crockpot—heavy, old, and well used—from the shelf where it had been stored since last winter and handed it to me. I wondered why she'd waited until now, why the act of cleaning had brought her back to that time so many years ago. The handles of the crockpot base had long ago broken off. I slid my hands underneath, beside hers, took it, and placed it on the counter by the sink. I kept bird feeders outside my window, filling them sporadically. If there wasn't a finch sitting on the plastic feeder at that moment, there should have been. Ellen leaned against the door jamb and looked out over the oven. Anywhere but at me.

"She said we wouldn't need her anymore, and she didn't want to be so alone. I don't know why she told me. What was I supposed to do? I don't think I ever said a word to you or Edwin about it, but it scared me pretty shitless."

No, Ellen never told me. I picture her that summer so many years ago, soon to graduate from college, a serious boyfriend, and now a mother she couldn't leave alone and a brother and sister she couldn't confide in.

"I checked for bullets in Daddy's guns we had in the house at the time. I tried to get Mama to talk more about it, but she wouldn't. All she said was that she had a will, and Aunt Peggy was the executor.

"Anyway, it was when we were under the 'don't talk about stuff' rule, so I couldn't have said anything even if I wanted to."

"I wouldn't have told her."

"You know what I mean."

Yes, I knew. Breaking our silence would have brought our walls tumbling down. But I didn't know then, and didn't care, what they both were going through. I wanted out, and I got out, not knowing what I'd left behind that summer. Nor did I fully understand Ellen's motivation that September when she insisted Mama see a psychologist in Greensboro. Ellen and I met her for dinner after her appointment.

"Waste of money," she snorted. "He told me I was lonely. I already knew that." She never went back.

CHAPTER 13

We five travelers spend our days together in the front and back seats of the van, our arms and knees pressing against others' arms and knees, or sharing console space in the front, one driving, one navigating. We eat meals together, talk over travel plans or destinations, occasionally stand together for a photograph, sometimes exploding in laughter. We follow our itinerary, and every evening after dinner, we retreat to our separate hotel rooms—and, in Edwin's case, sometimes a separate hotel—where we don't have to be polite, don't have to get along.

Day after day, Bill and I drag our suitcases into our room, choose our spaces for unloading and spreading out, though we don't spread out much, since we never spend more than two nights in any location. Night after night, I fall backwards onto the bed, relieved to be alone, and say without thinking, "It's going well so far, isn't it?"

And it is, he agrees, complaining just a little that he wishes we could choose better restaurants. I wonder out loud if Ellen's knee will hold up, if Edwin can keep up this nonstop pace. Day after day, night after night, I am exhausted but exhilarated. As Bill showers and settles into a book, I am wide awake, going over my notes and filling in journal pages about our days' activities. In his room in the hotel, Edwin is detailing Facebook posts with photos. Ellen, in hers, is icing her knee.

Traveling east from Brussels in the late afternoon, we arrive at the Hotel St. Martenslane in Maastricht in the Netherlands.

Called a "craft house," the St. Martenslane feels like a scene from HGTV—brightly colored rooms with sparse and ultramodern furniture. I chose Maastricht as a stop, because the 30th Infantry Division liberated it in the fall of 1944.

Maastricht has recovered well from war. The neighborhood surrounding the hotel is a lively area of shops and businesses, lightly scented with marijuana. For dinner, we choose a restaurant a few blocks from our hotel. I am diving into a side of bright green lettuce when my phone buzzes. Flashing on my screen is a number I've never seen and a message that reads, "Meet me at the entrance to the Margraten Cemetery. I am bringing my friend, who also loves the 30th Infantry. I am happy to finally meet you!"

I don't recognize the number, but I know who it is by the enthusiasm: Vince Heggen, tomorrow's guide. He's been the most energetic of our contacts and has often expressed his delight that we are coming.

I text back: "I'm looking forward to meeting you, but I don't know where the cemetery is."

Almost immediately, a reply arrives: "It's the famous cemetery near where you are staying. I thought we could start our day there."

"Yes, but how do we find it?"

Our navigation so far has been difficult. The van's GPS is like most I've ever used, taking us on unnecessary side trips and alleyways, including, in one case, a sidewalk. I thought I was being clever before we left America to print Google maps that would route us from hotel to hotel, but in reality, we rarely travel from hotel to hotel, so my paper maps are of little use.

"I will send you the directions beginning from your hotel," Vince replies.

More than a year earlier, I met Vince by clicking on an online web page about the making of a film about the 30th Infantry Division's victory in Mortain. Vince was listed as a resource and a war enthusiast from Belgium. He responded immediately to my email inquiry. He would show us all the important sites in southern Belgium and the Netherlands, he said, areas where much fighting occurred.

The next morning, using Vince's detailed instructions, we pull into the parking lot of the Margraten American Cemetery in the Netherlands, a fifteen-minute ride from our hotel. At 9:00 AM, the parking lot is full of cars but empty of people except two young men resting against the back bumper of a Saab sedan. I've never met Vince, but after our chatty emails, which he often closes with "Hugs, Vince," I feel as though we have known each other for years.

"We'll be the two crazy Belgian guys," he told me. "You'll know us when you see us."

I know him. His dark hair and eager eyes are distinctive, as his pictures portray him—fortyish, athletic, handsome, with a smile that relaxes the corners of his face. He is wearing stylish jeans and a royal blue hoodie, the shirttail of his checked shirt hanging below it.

"My friend, Marcel Verwilghen." Vince cups his hand on his companion's shoulder. "He loves the US like me. He also knows a lot about the war." Vince's Belgian sidekick has flung a dark blue sweater over his shoulder. He is pencil thin, with a close-cut gray-and-white beard and sun-dried skin. He looks to be several years older than Vince. If I weren't deep in the European countryside, I'd think Marcel was a Southern American good ol' boy—decked out in Levi jeans, a plaid shirt, cowboy boots, aviator sunglasses, and a camouflage-colored ball cap with an American eagle above the bill.

Then I do a double take. Edwin nudges my elbow, whispers, "See what he's wearing?"

Around his waist is a belt with a Confederate flag buckle, its blue-starred *X* set on red out of place in this Belgian countryside. Something in me lurches, stiffens. In my small town, the flag means trouble. Trucks with larger-than-life-sized stars and bars parade down Main Street, sometimes blaring "Dixie," which is rarely played except by those who don't care who it offends. I'm a southerner—all of us are, of course—and Bill, David, and Edwin especially love to study our southern history, including the Civil War. But unlike a few of our neighbors and fellow southerners, we understand the controversy the flag creates. To "flaggers," the symbol stands for heritage; to our Black friends and neighbors, it signifies centuries of oppression. We don't fly it, and we don't honor it.

"God Bless America" is piping softly through the cemetery's sound system. "This oughta be fun." Edwin shoots me a wink, grins, and then reaches out his hand in greeting. Marcel accepts it and squeezes hard, a wide smile on his face.

I fight to keep my eyes from falling to Marcel's belt buckle. As I greet Vince with the hug his emails have been asking for, Marcel's arms also open to me, so I hug him too.

"Yes, very good," he says with a laugh. The smile within his short beard is huge, and his eyes tell us he is delighted to be spending this day with children of an American GI.

The Margraten American Cemetery is the stunningly beautiful resting place for nearly eight thousand American soldiers who died on battlefields in Belgium and the Netherlands in late 1944 and early 1945. My glance inside the iron gate at row after row of crosses and Stars of David reminds me of the American Cemetery in Normandy. Unlike Normandy, this sacred ground has only a handful of visitors.

"As is true at Normandy and all battleground cemeteries, many Americans were not identified," Vince says, as we enter, pointing to a plaque dedicated to those soldiers whose bodies were never found or named. American flags fly above the graves and outside the memorial vaults.

We walk quietly through the rows, reading names and home states and pausing before those from my father's unit. I find myself lingering by the markers of North Carolina boys, wondering who they might have become if they'd had the chance to return home. I snap photos of the cross of a boy from the 120th regiment, twenty-three years old when he died; another, age thirty-five; others, nineteen or twenty.

Vince and Marcel pose for the camera, their arms around each other like brothers, in front of a cross from the 30th Infantry, row after row of white crosses and stars in the background. We stand in various arrangements, also posing, though it seems odd to smile.

"The people of Belgium and the Netherlands tend the graves," Vince tells us, walking on. "We place flowers on them on your Memorial Day and on other special occasions. We honor the men throughout the year by remembering what they did for us."

While we wait for David and Edwin to finish their cemetery walk, Vince, Marcel, Ellen, Bill, and I gather at the back gate, sharing stories. Vince has already written to me in an email that his grandfather sheltered American soldiers in his barn on the same property where he now tends the family apple orchard. His father, then a young boy, had befriended many soldiers, and last spring, Vince sent me a photograph of his father standing with a group.

"They were helping us, so my grandfather, of course, would help them," he says now. As a boy, he loved hearing stories told by his father and grandfather of the Americans. "I have been interested in the 30th Infantry as long as I remember. It's something I've known all my life."

"Marcel's mother," he says, touching his friend's shoulder, "was a child during the German occupation."

"She had long—," Marcel says, waving his fingers in a circle from his chin to his waist, searching for the word.

"Pigtails?" Ellen says.

"Yes, pigtails."

Vince steps in to help tell the story. One day, for spite, a German soldier cut off Marcel's mother's pigtails with his bayonet. His mother never forgot the incident and never forgave the soldier.

"That is why we love America," Marcel says, pausing between words to make sure he is using them correctly. "You gave us back our lives."

We follow Vince's Saab through lush countryside, and when he eases to the shoulder of the road near a small marker, we pull close behind him. Stepping from the car, he hands me a newspaper clipping, protected by a plastic sleeve, from the local paper, written in Dutch, dated 1944, and a second clipping a few days later, similar stories.

"I'm surprised that local papers were printed during the war," Bill says.

"Oh, yes," Vince responds. "Printing was sometimes unpredictable and sometimes secret, but much news was circulated and preserved." He points to the newspaper page. "This article tells of the first Americans killed in the liberation of the Netherlands," Vince says. "Both from your father's unit. I thought you would want to see where they died."

Their faces in the photographs are so young, the faces of boys. On the roadside, the stone memorial designates the place where the men were killed. Vince waits with Marcel beside his car while we take photos of the area where new spring greenery surrounds the reminder of deaths.

It is a crisp day, and the noon sun beams down. I am wearing a black fleece vest, which I slide off and tuck over my arm. Vince joins us by the marker.

"It's near lunchtime. Do you like Belgian fries?" he asks. Marcel, leaning against the Saab, smiles. "These are real fries, unlike French fries," Vince continues.

"I can't say I've ever had them," I say. "I'm game."

We speed along behind the Saab again, crossing the border into the province of Leige and finally to the village of Bassenge, turning in beneath a sign with bright blue lettering that reads, "Au Fistou Friterie Restaurant," above a fast-food place that reminds me of McDonald's or Chick-fil-A. At the counter inside, Vince orders one of each variety offered and two of some—fries with cheese, with spaghetti, with barbecue sauce, and more. We carry them to tables and spread out, sampling fries from each. I have tasted Canadian poutine—fries with cheese drenched with brown gravy—but the thick, crispy potatoes of the friterie are a new experience. Vince and Marcel are glowing and passing plates to make sure we sample them all. They are delicious, thick, warm, and filling.

As plates begin to empty, Vince asks, "Would you like to visit Fort Eben-Emael after lunch? There's a one o'clock tour in English."

I glance at my watch. Already it's past twelve-thirty. I would love to see the fort, I tell him. It has earned a full page in my father's journal, including a *Stars and Stripes* clipping about its capture.

Our father kept a large Nazi flag in a box on a lower shelf of the bookcase with his other memorabilia. He always told us he took it from a fort. Every summer when we were growing up, we draped the flag, as large as a dining room tablecloth or a bed sheet across three clotheslines for airing. Sometimes during those summer days, we imagined low-flying planes on reconnaissance over our back yard or anticipated a knock on the door by someone objecting to our displaying it so publicly.

"Do you think the flag in our collection might have come from Eben-Emael?" I ask.

"Very likely," Vince says. The German domination was weakening, he continues, and GIs were grabbing souvenirs wherever they could find them. Chances are many soldiers brought home Nazi flags that later aired on suburban clotheslines.

We follow Vince's Saab down the curvy road to Eben-Emael. Thirty minutes later and past one o'clock, we arrive at the fort, though all we can see is a cave-like entrance and a mound of grass.

Vince chats with the ticket-office clerk, attempting to arrange a private excursion. His attempt fails. "The English tour is already underway. Another tour starts at two," he tells us when he returns. "It's in French, but you can join if you want."

"Of course," I say, speaking for us all, imagining a quick thirty-minute run-through, and we'll be on our way. At least we'll get to see inside.

Ellen's knee is killing her, she admits when I lean close and ask. No, she doesn't need a doctor, she insists, though the joint remains swollen. The brace she bought at a Saint-Lô pharmacy after we stopped in the village for food is tight around her leg, and she is regularly dosing with ibuprofen.

I am beginning to understand how much she wants to be on this trip. She missed Fox Red, and she doesn't want to lose another opportunity to see what the rest of us are seeing, to trace every inch of this journey. No one is angrier than Ellen at her injury a few days ago. As is her style, she'll power through and not complain. She doesn't say it, but I wonder if she's afraid she'll slow the rest of us down or keep us from doing what we have come here to do. She wants to go in, she tells me. We turn toward the dark entrance where the guards wait.

Vince gives us a quick history of Fort Eben-Emael, which sits on the Belgium-German border at the Albert Canal and was built in the late 1930s by Belgians as a defense against the impending

German advance. It was the largest, strongest fort of its kind, accommodating up to twelve hundred soldiers. That's a lot of soldiers in an underground rabbit warren.

Similar to the failed Maginot Line, built after World War I by the French to be an impenetrable barrier against German attack—which was quickly breached by Hitler's troops in 1940—Eben-Emael was intended as a formidable defense for Belgium.

In 1941, German gliders quietly landed on the fort's grassy dome without detection and dropped a bomb into the ventilation hole, opening it wide enough so that soldiers could rush in, taking the Belgian army completely by surprise. Eighty-five German soldiers and twenty minutes were all it took to capture the fort, a crushing defeat for Belgians.

Three years of intense war followed. In late 1944, American forces pushed across France into Belgium, headed straight for the fort. By this time, the end of German domination across Europe was in sight. Instead of staying to defend the fort, German soldiers, fearing the worst, fled. Our father was one of the American soldiers who recaptured the fort for the Allies.

It's difficult to describe the interior of Fort Eben-Emael. It's a colossal cave in absolute darkness except for artificial lights strung across low ceilings. Damp. Cold. Claustrophobic. Airless. To be a soldier trapped in that underground cavern might be worse than being inside a steel tank, worse than an open-air battlefield. There is no way out once that steel front door closes.

It doesn't look like much from the outside and doesn't look large. A concrete entrance, that reminds me of coal mines I've seen in Kentucky, is semi-hidden within a grass-covered hill. Inside, the fort is dark and musty with years and the suggestion of stale sweat of long-ago soldiers. We hurry down the first hallway to join the tour group, which has paused at the first intersection not far from the entrance. The guide glances toward us, nods as though welcoming us, and continues his talk in clear, fast French. Bill, listening hard to retrieve words from his high school language class, nods now and then to show understanding, but the rest of us hover near the rear.

The group walks, pauses to listen to a story by the guide, and then walks on. Sometimes they laugh and chat with one another. Occasionally someone will glance back to where we five Americans are dragging behind, Vince following another six feet back from us. Every now and then he'll catch up and translate.

"He's telling about the German takeover of 1941." Vince points to a section of the ceiling with rough patching that looks to be seventy-plus years old. "Here's where the Germans landed in their gliders, took the fort completely by surprise. You can see the ventilation hole, where it was patched. A single explosive. It's amazing, isn't it, that that's all it took."

Our tour guide, a middle-aged man wearing the uniform of a soldier, or perhaps, I think, of a national park ranger, loves to talk, and offers in-depth responses to visitors' questions. We wait, peeking in iron-gated doorways or reading signage. I'm ready for the tour to end, which, I convince myself, will be any minute.

Thirty minutes pass. Ellen nudges me, motions to a hallway and a room filled with artifacts—helmets, medals, swords, uniforms and more. "This is a lot more interesting than listening to him," she says.

We ease away from the others, David close behind, and enter the display room, keeping one eye on the group, so we won't be left behind. We're viewing the helmets, weaponry, and other artifacts when we hear a harsh, "Madam! Madam!" We turn. A uniformed guard hastens toward us. "You must not be in here. You must stay with the group." His English is sharp-edged. He means business.

"We were just looking," Ellen says. "Is this okay?"

"No, not okay. You must go back to the group."

Sheepishly, we look toward the small gathering, their backs to us now as they push forward following the guide. Edwin, who has begun walking toward us, stops.

"The tour comes back to this place," says the guard. "But you cannot be here by yourselves."

We both mumble, "Sorry," and, feeling more than a bit guilty, walk back to our group.

On a wall in the hallway is a sign that reads, "Verboten!" It does not say what is forbidden, but the word is threatening. The damp walls of the fort are watching us, so it seems, and something about the place makes me want to obey.

An hour into our Eben-Emael tour, no end is in sight. What my father and his men accomplished in thirty minutes—a full flushing out of the fort—is taking our entire afternoon.

"We'll get through this," Ellen whispers, I think as much to herself as to me. We are edgy and tired. Ellen's limp seems more pronounced, and every so often, I see her wince, or maybe it's me, wincing for her. At each turn, I think we'll be heading out of the fort, but instead, we embark down another long, stony hallway. Two hours become three.

Fort Eben-Emael is creepy for another reason: it's been restaged as a German-occupied fort, not American or Belgian. In the officers' quarters, mannequins in German uniforms sit around large tables studying maps; in the enlisted men's quarters, mannequins perch on the edges of cots, polishing their boots; in the mess hall, they gather to eat; in the infirmary, they lie on beds, wrapped in bandages, what looks like dried blood on their heads or arms or legs. It's unnerving, especially in the dim light, within the concrete walls.

Deeper and deeper we walk through the dark tunnels of the fort, following the group that follows the guide who talks on and on in French. Edwin sometimes appears interested, though his frequent glances and eye rolls reveal frustration and boredom. Bill continues to listen, picking up words here and there. David wanders, but not far, because the "Madam! Madam!" assistant walks at the rear, keeping an eye on us.

It isn't as though we can go anywhere anyway. We have turned down so many hallways, we could never find our way out on our own. All we can do is keep going. I watch Ellen, who is moving more and more slowly. Every few minutes she reaches down and massages her swollen knee.

I glance at my watch: three and a half hours have passed.

We follow the group through a narrow passageway that now winds up a set of steep steel stairs into the gunnery rooms. "Can I wait down here?" Ellen asks Vince, who shakes his head. He has done this tour many times before. "We won't come back this way. Up is the only way out." While the others climb with the group, she pauses on the second landing. "Go on past," she says. "I'll get there." I move ahead but only by a few steps.

The higher we climb, the tighter the space, and oddly, the staler the air. We pause while the guide talks. "This has to be the end," I whisper to Ellen. Instead, we start up another flight, another spiral staircase. The air grows hotter. Ellen's face is pinched and red, but she perseveres. She doesn't complain.

After the third gunnery room, the group marches forward and the guide quits talking.

"That's it," says Vince. He turns down the hallway until we can see daylight. Ahead is the ticket booth, the main entrance, and a small group gathering at the opening, perhaps for the next tour.

I could have said no to this excursion, and perhaps should have. But even in another language, in just seeing the place, I've learned more about the German army and the reputation of the American forces earned in a few short months of fighting. I have learned about endurance, relief, and the unpredictability of war and war journeys.

And I have learned about my sister. She's strong. She doesn't complain. She takes her time, breathing deeply, favoring the bad knee, only now and then grimacing or placing her hand on the wall. I walk a few feet behind her, always her shadow, as she steps into the afternoon sun.

CHAPTER 14

I like Marcel. He's full of energy, and when he walks, he bounces, the heels of his boots lifting off the ground. He pays attention with his eyes, which are a soft brown gray like his hair. I understand few of his words, so Vince translates. Smiles are frequent among us all, and Marcel's is welcoming and warm. I try not to let my gaze fall to the Stars and Bars belt buckle that continues to catch my attention like a rogue fireworks display.

"Marcel wants you to see his museum," Vince says, as we return to the parking lot. Earlier, Vince described his own "museum," which is what he calls his collection of World War II uniforms, weaponry, and equipment. "We'll go by his house, take a rest, and he'll show you what he has. His is not as large as mine, but he has some nice pieces."

We follow the Saab through business districts and residential developments until we stop in front of a modest house in a neighborhood where cars line the sides of the street and people sit on porches or work in their yards. It's like a scene from a 1950s movie. Marcel jumps from the Saab and escorts us down the sidewalk, talking as we head to the door. "He is sorry his wife is not home," Vince translates. "She was excited to meet you too and wanted to be here."

"Please, please," Marcel says in hesitant English, outstretching his arm and motioning us to a living area where a half dozen chairs circle a table. "I make you something to drink."

We sit while he and Vince disappear to the kitchen and return a few minutes later with a tray of cold glasses. "Marcel thinks you would like to have some Coke." Vince sets the tray on the table.

"Coke." Marcel beams. "Like in America." We laugh and reach for glasses, while our two hosts sit awkwardly on the edge of the couch nearby, unsure of how to entertain us or what to say. When our glasses are empty but for a few swallows, Marcel stands. "Now would you like to see my museum?"

I am amused by Marcel's nervous hospitality, but I'm also humbled by it. I don't know when I've felt so important to anyone. He leads us down the hallway to what looks like an extra bedroom and opens the door. I wonder if his wife insists he keep it closed the way I shut the door to Bill's office, stacked high with old newspapers.

Mannequins in authentic olive or khaki World War II uniforms stand, sit, or kneel in front of a sandbag wall. The room is staged to resemble a bunker, with netting and canvas tarps hanging as backdrop, mess kits and other personal items dangling from flaps. The lifelike soldiers hold guns or canteens, and on their heads, helmets sit loosely, as they would for a young man barely old enough for war. In addition, American flags line the walls, and other war memorabilia—boots, packs, parachutes, tents—are tucked into or opened onto every available space. Marcel puffs his chest and puts his arm around Vince and then Edwin as the rest of us take photos. His pride in his collection and his staging is endearing. More than once now he has said, "I love America," and I believe him, but I'm not sure what loving America means to him.

"We find our museum pieces online," Vince says, answering my question before I ask. "There are many sites and auctions. So many family members who don't want the stuff anymore. We get good prices. If it's too high, we bargain or we won't buy."

History feeds both men's desire to preserve the paraphernalia of war. But something else inspires them. Though the mannequins don't have names, their uniforms, packs, canteens once belonged to individual soldiers, their stories kept alive here.

A good museum brings its subject to life, whether it contains artifacts from a war or replicas of a Cherokee village, a monument to someone's legacy or a shoe, a jacket, or a helmet, enough to spark a personal memory. Marcel's museum honors the memory, the soldiers, and the war in a way I understand because it brings human history to life. It puts the gun in the hands of a single boy—never mind that these boys are mannequins, their eyes vacant, bodies fixed in time.

Our father's collection is a museum also, I realize. It's taken years for me to understand that behind his musty journals and scrapbooks, lists of names and photographs of men all wearing the same uniform who look the same, except for a pair of glasses or a mustache, are personal stories of war. My history studies in classrooms for the most part have been delivered as dates and facts. My father visited high school classes with his collection of helmets. He told stories of friends, associating faces with the war so that students could grasp its significance more easily than they could with just facts and dates. That's what Marcel's museum is doing, telling personal stories, even with mannequins. Living history.

The clock reads almost five o'clock by the time we leave Marcel's house, but the sun won't set until after nine tonight, so we have plenty of daylight hours.

"We'll make one more stop and then go to my house," Vince says. "I want you to see the Henri-Chapelle Cemetery. I think you will like it very much."

Vince and Marcel are spry as fawns, and I get the feeling they would show us sites as long as we are willing to keep going, but I'm not sure how much longer we're good for. I check in with the

other travelers, reading faces and body language for tiredness or dis-
interest. Bill gives me a thumb's up, letting me know he's fine. Ellen
and David are chatting together, but when she sees me, she nods to
let me know they want to keep going. A glance at Edwin worries
me: his face is red and moist with sweat. Still, he shoots me a grin,
and I set aside worries.

Bill drives, following Vince's Saab, and David sits beside him
in the passenger seat. Edwin, Ellen, and I slide into the back. Late
afternoon has grown warm, sun melting in the sky, and after sitting
in direct sunlight with windows closed, the van is steamy. Bill turns
the air conditioner on high, but it doesn't help cool the back seat.
Edwin has dropped his head onto the side window, and his eyes are
closed.

"Are you all right?" Ellen, sitting beside him, asks.

He opens his eyes and closes them again. "I don't know what's
come over me. I'm dizzy, hot. I feel like I did when I had my kidney
stone."

She turns to me, squinches her eyes in worry or frustration, I'm
not sure. "Are you still taking your antibiotics?" she asks.

"Finished them this morning."

"Why don't you stay in the car at the cemetery? Don't push
yourself," I say.

"No, no." He takes a deep breath, an audible breath, and lifts his
head from the glass. "I want to go. Just let me close my eyes. I'm so
thirsty. I could use some water."

"We've got bottles in the back," I say. "When we stop, I'll get
you one." He blows out a long breath and rests his head on the
window for the twenty-minute ride to the cemetery. Ellen gives me
a what-do-we-do look I remember from childhood when he was
getting the better of us, but we refused to let him win. I return the
look without an answer, because I don't have one. Will he need a
doctor? A hospital? My frustration shifts to concern. I'm sure this is

not what Vince is expecting, either. I'd like to keep our guide from suspecting anything's wrong, but if Edwin needs medical assistance, Vince can help us get it.

Ahead, the Henri-Chapelle American Cemetery rises up on the horizon, its stark white stone markers like seagulls paused in grass beneath a blue sky. As we pull into the parking lot, I am startled by its beauty. Perhaps my response to Henri-Chapelle is due in part to late afternoon sun that sweeps over the graves, highlighting the white crosses and Stars of David and casting long shadows in grass to form a stunning, holy place. Perhaps my response is that we have spent the day studying war, and the cemetery is the most humbling reminder of the war's cost to ordinary people. We began the morning impressed and respectful, but now at day's end, I can only be silent, awed by the power and certainty of death.

"I'll join you in a minute," Edwin says. He sits with the van door open, one foot out resting on the ground, sipping a lukewarm bottle of water. "Tell Vince I'm fine." I'm not convinced, but I leave him there, catch up with the others, and enter through the cemetery gates.

Similar in numbers to the Normandy American Cemetery and the Margraten American Cemetery, this fifty-seven-acre plot of precisely arranged white marble within a perfectly groomed field is the final resting place for almost eight thousand men, and an additional 450 unknown soldiers. It feels even more sacred than the other two cemeteries. Perhaps it's the stark white columns or the sloping hillside of markers. Perhaps it's the angel holding a branch who looks down from a sky-high pedestal.

As we pace through the cemetery, up and down its straight and tragic rows, Vince zeros in on soldiers from the 30th Infantry. He pauses by the stones of graves he has adopted—over thirty in all, he tells us—lingering on names, telling stories. One is familiar.

"Lt. Col. Paul McCollum." Vince steps forward, close enough to read the name, too far away to touch.

Earlier in our email correspondence, Vince had asked me if the name meant anything to me. It did. My father mentions McCollum several times in his journal, including his leadership in the capture of Fort Eben-Emael.

"He was much beloved," Vince tells us. "Many veterans who have come to see us stop at this grave. They remember what a great man he was."

I've heard the name so often that I feel as though I'm visiting the grave of a family friend. McCollum was from High Point, North Carolina, twenty minutes from my current home in Lexington, thirty minutes from the house where my father grew up. My father's scrapbook includes a photograph of the lieutenant colonel during a pause in the march through France, sitting on a log, his helmet un-buckled, looking squarely into the camera, not smiling, the sobriety of war numbing his expression. The cross brings home to me his death, the loss of a son to a family so close in geography to my own. A man my father admired.

To have opened and closed this day with these humbling cem-eteries was a brilliant plan on Vince's part. We've seen battle sites, we've heard stories of courage, but I realize, as I stand in this late afternoon sun in this most beautiful cemetery of all, that Vince's stories are what has made the war real to us today. He's given names to brothers, sons, and husbands. How but through a stroke of luck did our father, just another brother and son, not end up beneath one of these white crosses? How near to his heart was a bullet or a bomb, we'll never know. We're surrounded by death, and each name on each stone means not just a life lost but a family destroyed, a family not begun.

I turn when I see Edwin walking toward us. He's clinging to his bottle of water with only an inch remaining. He isn't racing, but a bounce has returned to his step.

"I think I just needed something to drink," he announces to us all. "I must have been dehydrated." His face is flushed, and he might not be telling us everything he is feeling, but he's up, he's here.

We arrive at Vince's house in Fouron le Comte situated within a few minutes of the cemetery. To the left of his front door hangs a metal plaque, twice the size of a mailbox, the Old Hickory blue and red emblem in its center, commemorating the death of First Sergeant Wallace J. Horton, Company A, 119th Infantry. Vince tells us his story: only nineteen years old, Horton was killed by machine-gun fire at a crossroads while his company was liberating a village. He is buried in the Henri-Chapelle Cemetery, and Vince has adopted his grave. To honor the soldier and remember his sacrifice, Vince has fixed the commemorative plaque in a place where he will see it multiple times each day.

Vince operates the generations-old family apple orchard, and on most days, he has told me, he is too busy to take an entire day off. We are lucky that he's between harvests right now. No apple trees are visible from the house, but the scent of apples surrounds us.

"Being with you is important," he told me when I first contacted him. "It is what I want to do." We step inside, and Vince's wife, Carine, and his three daughters, Laura, Adeline, and Eva greet us. Dogs, cats, a rabbit, fish, and more critters roam freely throughout the house or gaze out from their glass containers.

"The Heggen girls love animals," Carine tells us, smiling. "So, Vince and I do too." The youngest Heggen daughter, Eva, cuddles a brown rabbit in her arms and holds it up to show to Ellen.

"We used to have rabbits, too," Ellen says, rubbing the soft ears.

Eva takes my hand and leads me to the side yard, where she hops onto the trampoline to demonstrate her practiced flips and high jumps. Her long, dark hair flies into the air above her, and her loose, brightly colored pants dance around her legs. I take a few pictures, which seems to delight her. Her excitement is endearing.

"Time to eat!" Carine calls. Eleven of us gather around a long table in the great room, sipping beers and passing boxes of pizza. At one point, Eva slides from her chair at the end of the table and scribbles on a chalkboard in the living area.

"Come see," she says, taking my hand. In large letters, she's written, "Welcome, USA," and has drawn the Old Hickory logo. I'm intrigued to think that she might know more about the 30th Infantry Division than I knew a few months ago and certainly more than most, if not all, American children.

"Thank you so much! I love it!" I say. She smiles. She's changed clothes and now sports blue and pink pants. I wonder how many times a day she changes.

"Where's Marcel?" Edwin asks. Without our noticing, our second guide has disappeared from the room.

"He'll be back," Vince says. "He has a surprise for you." He smiles at Carine, who seems to be in on whatever surprise Marcel and Vince have cooked up.

I look around the table at my family and Vince's. Ellen is deep in conversation with Carine and smiling, sharing stories of their daughters. Edwin and David are talking with Vince about the orchard and Vince's apple business.

Here we are in Belgium, I think, having dinner with the grandson of someone who might have met my father. It feels unbelievable. Edwin looks my way with a smile that suggests perhaps he knows what I am thinking. Our families were strangers until a few hours ago, and yet they've opened their home to us, and I feel as if we've known the Heggen family forever.

A roar, like an airplane overhead or large fan blades slicing air, grows louder outside the kitchen. It rumbles to a stop, and the side kitchen door swings wide. Marcel enters, pausing at the threshold. He's wearing the uniform of a 1944 30th Infantry Division soldier, from jacket to pants to cap. On his shoulder is the Old Hickory emblem patch and beneath it, sergeant's stripes. A grin stretches across his face.

"Come outside and see the real surprise." Vince pushes open the kitchen door, signaling us to follow. In the driveway, parked in front of the Wallace J. Horton plaque, is a vintage olive-green 1944 Willys Jeep, a white star painted on its hood, identification numbers on the sides, front and back seats empty, and no windows or rooftop.

"Unbelievable!" says Edwin. We laugh loudly, delighted as much by Marcel's joy in sharing his jeep with us as the jeep itself.

Marcel stands beside it like a new father. "Please, sit," he says.

"Is it okay?" I ask. Edwin edges forward, his hand on the front bumper. He climbs in the driver's seat, Ellen beside him, and I step into the rear seats.

"If you'd like, he'll take you for a ride," Vince says. It's almost nine o'clock, but it's still light. I hesitate, knowing we have an early start and a full day tomorrow, but I look at my brother's and sister's faces. They are children, all smiles.

The jeep will only hold three passengers plus a driver, so Marcel slides into position behind the wheel, and Edwin and Ellen shift to the back seat, giving me the front and best view. I climb in, holding on to the side windshield like I've seen soldiers in movies do, my foot resting by the door.

Vince, his daughter Adeline, David, and Bill follow in the Saab as Marcel drives us along beautiful country roads, through lush patches of trees, casting long shadows in the late evening sun and then up hills, down hills, and around curves. The three of us are whooping and laughing as though we are on a roller coaster, evening air slapping our faces, blowing our hair. Finally, Marcel pulls up to a stone gate. The jeep's engine putters as we ease through it into a courtyard and stop.

"The Mheer Castle," says Vince, walking toward us as we climb out. The fourteenth-century castle, nestled in the village of Mheer in the Netherlands has no connection with the war, he explains, but it is a beautiful part of his region's history. The majestic stone home with four cornering turrets sits at the top of a hill, perfect for keeping watch in its fortress days. We walk the grounds and view the landscape beyond the high walls that surround the courtyard.

Darkness is complete when Bill, Edwin, and Adeline change places with us in the jeep for the slower, quieter ride back to Vince's house. We have only one more stop, Vince reminds us. Back at the house, before we leave, we must see his museum.

A large United States flag greets us at the entrance to the curated space in his basement. As with Marcel's museum, life-sized mannequins in uniform stand or sit in corners or against walls. The accoutrements of war fill every available space. Buttons, medals, patches, and more line glass-covered display cases, and weapons are mounted on walls, hung on racks, or positioned in soldiers' hands. Three adjoining rooms are full—yes, it is a mini-museum. Even more than Marcel's collection, which is small by comparison, these rooms do, in fact, tell stories of war.

"I've gathered signatures on my flag of all the 30th Infantry soldiers who have come through," Vince says. I step closer and realize that the white stripes of the flag are filled with names written in many colors of ink. "I would be proud if you sign for your father." Vince hands Edwin a pen. My brother turns his baseball cap backwards, bends low, and carefully prints our father's name and service information in the first white stripe beneath the square of fifty stars and then signs his own name below it.

It's been an extraordinary day, better than I ever imagined we might have when we left Maastricht this morning, unsure where we were headed. I watch my brother, on his knees. My sister looks over his shoulder, her hand on her cheek.

Marcel stands back, his arms folded across his chest, that familiar stance. My eyes fall for the last time to his belt buckle, barely visible behind the flaps of his 30th Infantry jacket.

"I love America," he says, as though reading my thoughts. Or perhaps he is remarking on Edwin, one more soldier's child, alive to write a name on this fabric. "I love everything American." I glance at my new friend's genuine eyes and return his smile.

CHAPTER 15

My first-year college boyfriend, Rick, was a tall, skinny nineteen-year-old with hair that fell below his shoulders and a beard that peaked below his chin, making him look slightly devilish. He had a nervous habit of chirping like a bird by shooting air between his teeth. Most of the time he didn't realize he was doing it, and I shushed him to keep him from embarrassing himself or me.

Mama first met him on the evening she visited me in my dorm room after a meeting on campus, which was also her alma mater. When she arrived, he was in my room, lying across my bed while I studied at my desk. He bounded up, pulled out a chair for her, and introduced himself. His presence was a complete surprise, but she was friendly, if not flirtatious, something I'd noticed she'd been practicing.

"He's all right, but I wish he didn't have all that hair," my mother said whenever I mentioned Rick. "He's all right" was as far as she would go to admitting she liked any of my boyfriends. Later she used the same line about my half-chow, half-lab dog.

In April, Rick and I decided to drive home from Greensboro to attend the annual Faculty Follies at my old high school. The Follies was a student council fundraiser where faculty members showed off talents like singing or piano playing or teamed up to entertain students by doing skits or other acts. My mother had been practicing with the Spanish teacher to perform a duo in the follies. That's all she told me when she called and said she'd like it if I were to come. We both were trying to be nicer to each other—I had begun to think that she too might have had a rough few years, and my attitude wasn't making it any better.

Mama was one of two guidance counselors at the school, her specialty getting students into college. When I told her we'd be there, the first thing she said was, "Has he had a haircut?"

"We'll sit in the back," I said. I wasn't excited about being back at the high school I disliked so much, and I hoped to slip in and out without seeing any old teachers or younger classmates.

We were late, and the house lights were dim and the stage lit when we sneaked in the auditorium door. We excused our way to two empty seats in the center about halfway down.

According to the program, Mama's performance with Mr. Jarrett, the short, pudgy, bald Spanish teacher, better known throughout the school as Señor Jarrett, was in the second half of the follies. When the heavy curtains on stage parted, I felt like a spotlight was on me with my long-haired boyfriend, back in a place I had hated throughout high school. Enjoying the show became easy, and Rick, knowing my discomfort, kept his arm around my shoulder. I couldn't help but laugh at the male coaches, dressed as cheerleaders and leading the audience in a round of the school fight song, ending with "Go, Blue Comets!" It's the same show the coaches did year after year, and even though they looked ridiculous, they'd end up being one of the most popular acts, for no other reason than they were the coaches.

When Mr. Fairley, my favorite science teacher, stepped onto stage in a cowboy outfit, complete with chaps, a red bandanna, boots, and a stick for a horse, the laughter shifted. He was much beloved but was also awkward, absent-minded, and overly in love with chemistry. It wasn't that his voice was bad or his performance sub-par; it was that in trying not to be funny, he was hilarious. The audience, still laughing after the coaches' cheers, was ready to laugh more.

When he gave a little bow and began to sing, "They Call the Wind Maria," I could tell by the sincerity with which he raised his arms toward an imaginary Western sky that this wasn't going to go well. He punctuated his singing by sweeping his arm across what must have been the wind then taking off his cowboy hat and placing it against his chest. Laughter that had begun to die down was building again, and it was throwing him off. You aren't supposed to be laughing, his face said. After what felt like a slow hour but was no more than five minutes, Mr. Fairley finished and made his way offstage, his shoulders slumped.

During the short intermission that followed, Rick and I stayed in our seats until the second half of the show began. One of the Spanish teachers, a bell-shaped mother of two, along with the drama teacher, a single man who was a recent college graduate and overly enthusiastic about everything, performed the Mexican hat dance around a sombrero they'd centered on stage. They crossed their arms over their chests and kicked their feet in the air. They were electric with energy and fun.

My mother and Señor Jarrett were next. I had no idea what they had planned, but I knew they'd practiced to the point that she was surprisingly not as nervous as I was. "He'll be the star," she said. "I'm just giving him a chance to shine." He'd be the comedian, as he always was; her role was the straight man sidekick.

Mama stepped out first, entering the stage from behind the left side of the burgundy curtain. She was wearing a long, black wig with square cut bangs across her forehead and a mini-skirt that stopped well above her knees.

The music began, a familiar musical intro—"DUH-duh-duh-duh-duh-duh" that I recognized immediately.

She swayed her bony hips slightly, holding a silenced microphone, and she began lip-syncing words to the music, flipping her black hair over her shoulder. Then Cher's voice piped in with the opening lines of "I Got You, Babe," her love song to Sonny and his to her, the story of their youth, of everyone's doubt that their love would last. Mama as Cher gazed lovingly to the opposite curtain, from which stepped Mr. Jarrett, his arm reaching for her like a long-lost lover, coming for her in over-dramatized big steps, lip-syncing his response to the doubters, his love for Cher.

His wig, sitting slightly crooked on his bald head, was solid black and bowl-shaped. Beads bounced against his black T-shirt that hung loosely over his rounding belly and over a pair of striped bell-bottoms. She was almost a head taller than he was. They met in the middle, clasped hands, and she gazed down into his eyes. He mouthed the words, she mouthed the words, as articulately into their microphones as if they were belting out the lyrics, while the recorded music from the famous duo filled the auditorium.

The audience roared. Yes, this short, pudgy Spanish teacher, a single man of forty, was funny, exaggerated, and completely comfortable in his ridiculous role. But here was the somewhat recently widowed guidance counselor, pushing fifty but still with a Cher-like body, doing something I always knew she had in her—being funny. Having fun. It was so incongruous and so wonderful that I was on my feet, clapping, by the time they got to the first "I got you, babe" chorus.

They danced around stage, singing. She flipped her hair, he flipped his right back, and occasionally it slipped from its perch and he had to reposition it, which he did, of course, with great drama. She swayed, he swayed. They looked lovingly into each other's eyes. If it had been anyone except Mama and Mr. Jarrett, a person might wonder if something was going on between them, but those who knew better—pretty much everyone in that auditorium—knew what was happening here wasn't about love. It was about a woman so sad she could barely rise from bed in the morning being drawn out of herself by the antics of a genuine, caring friend.

When I heard a chorus rising up from the back of the auditorium, calling her name—"Tina! Tina!"—I knew the yearbook staff members were chanting their support. For the last two years, she had been advising the staff, with whom she spent a lot of late afternoon and some weekend hours laying out pages and editing.

The audience was standing with Rick and me, and by the last line, everyone was singing along with them. "I got you, babe. I got you, babe." After the last line, as the final notes of the recording played out, Mr. Jarrett took her in his arms and dipped her into a backwards swoon that seemed to surprise even her.

Rick squeezed my hand. They exited stage, returned for a final bow, and were gone. The audience cheered one last time before sitting.

I knew that something miraculous had happened, something transformative, and I don't remember seeing another single act in the follies that night.

My mother was beginning to breathe. Her long nightmare was not over, but joy, for one evening and offered up by a cute but lumpy Spanish teacher, had taken her for a spin.

She began to reinvent herself after that, slowly but intentionally. She joined the country club, took up golf, made new, single friends she could go out with at night. She signed up for a makeover at our local department store. She shopped for apartments in Greensboro, where she planned to start over. She joined a group called Parents Without Partners and the singles group at church. She went to dances, dinners. Eventually men started coming to the house to pick her up for dates. Ellen and I checked them out on occasional weekends when we were home from college. While she finished getting ready, we interrogated them, asking about jobs, children, how they liked to spend their time. They were professional men with college degrees and successful careers. Divorced men, widowers. Men with children. Men without. They entered our house like it was a fashion show runway, and they were on display. Not a single man who came to the house reminded me of my father. I was thrilled for her, and so was Ellen. Edwin, who had not lived with her through the hard years, who had not seen her at her worst, was less sure.

Her return to life didn't happen overnight, of course, but she knew what she was doing. She needed to save herself. Maybe after saving herself, I thought, she would throw a lifeline to us.

That November over Thanksgiving weekend, Mama insisted that Ellen and I join her on a bus trip to Florida with her teacher friends. "It'll be fun," she said. "Something different. Good for us all." I was angry because I had to go, and I was bored because that was the best way I knew to express my anger. Besides Ellen and me, the only young person on the bus was the daughter of our driver who was also the high school football coach and, on this trip, the tour director. The girl slept the entire ride to Florida in the far back seat, stumbling down the bus steps at rest stops, her long hair tangling in all directions. I suspected she was coming down from another kind of trip, which, knowing what we knew about her, she probably was.

On Saturday morning, the bus unloaded in the parking lot at Disney World in Orlando where we spent the day walking, seeing shows, and eating at sidewalk cafes while watching princesses and Mickey Mouses as they strolled by. I refused to admit I was having a good time. Late afternoon, Mama threw her arm around the Big Bad Wolf's shoulders, cocked her hip, and posed. She was smiling, holding on tight to the wolf as though he was the man she'd been wanting all these years. Her round sunglasses hid the dark circles beneath her eyes. She was pencil thin, bony, like the wolf.

"We've got time for one more ride," Ellen said, checking the clock above the tower of the Magic Kingdom. The tour bus would pick us up at the entrance at exactly six o'clock that evening, and we didn't want to hold up the others. Tomorrow we'd head back to our regular lives, driving the long highway from Disney World to North Carolina in one long road trip.

Ellen snapped a picture of the Big Bad Wolf as he kissed Mama on the cheek, and she feigned anger.

"Does she seem happy?" Ellen sidled up beside me. "I'm so glad we came."

"That makes one of us," I whispered.

"At least try."

"I am."

"Try harder. We're at Disney World, after all."

She was right, and it had been a fun day, the three of us splashing down the chute on the log rides, which we climbed into over and over despite the long lines. All three of us screamed with glee when the spray of water soaked us. We'd ducked into stage shows to watch singing bears and dancing alligators. In my shoulder purse, I carried a just-purchased Alice in Wonderland mug and a pair of socks I'd wear with my boots when we got home. I'd forgotten to be angry.

"This way," Mama said, and we followed her down the avenue, leaving the Big Bad Wolf trying to comfort a small, terrified girl. We stopped at the end of a line that seemed to be moving fast. "I could sit down for a few minutes," she said, "and this will do it."

We climbed into the bumper boats of the "It's a Small World" river float that took us around the globe one country at a time. Air was cool inside the cavern. Our boat was just large enough for the three of us, and when we went around river bends, bouncing off the rubber sides of the river, water splashed the edges of our boat and pooled at our feet.

Quietly, watching and listening, we cruised through Antarctica, Iceland, Russia. With each country we passed, a spotlight popped on, zeroing in on an animated child from that country, maybe a Dutch girl or a boy from South America, a Japanese girl or a dark-skinned African boy. The river through the cavern reminded me of fourth grade when we learned world history by studying its children. A good memory, a happy time. Now, children from all countries in the world sang the same lilting melody in the words of their native language, and it put me at ease.

Around curves, through tunnels, into green jungles and desert sands, the boat drifted on. The longer we rode, the more the song fixed in my head: "It's a small world, after all," high pitched, happy, not a care. I glanced at Mama, who looked longingly at the children, as though she was imagining herself in another life.

It ended too soon. "We've got time to do it again," Ellen said. "We're real close to where we meet the bus." We rejoined the line, inching forward until the crew hands held the boat steady for us to step in. Around the world again we went, children singing, dancing, water splashing in.

I didn't want to get back on the bus, didn't want to leave this place. Perhaps there was a kind of magic here, I wanted to believe, casting spells, helping us for one day to pretend we lived in a Disney world where anything was possible, all dreams come true. Or maybe something else had grabbed us, carried us away, like happiness on repeat, a flow to drift into, knowing someone else was navigating. We didn't have to be ourselves here. We didn't have to think about what we'd left at home. And Mama was happy, and Ellen was happy, here, in this imaginary place, and even I was happy.

We were the last ones to climb the steps to the bus, its engine already rumbling and ready to be put into gear for the trip back to the hotel. Sitting at the front, in the seat behind her driver-father, the tripped-out daughter was awake, alert, and she was smiling, and I wondered if she too had found some magic.

CHAPTER 16

Livingston was a Second Air Division veteran of World War II who saw no action because of an ear problem detected during his physical exam. On their first date, he told my mother, "I'm going to marry you."

"You are not," she said. She surprised us all, and perhaps even herself, a year later by saying yes.

What I remember most about their July wedding was how happy she was, how happy we all were. She wore a pale blue dress with a pleated skirt, a perfect complement to her dark hair, just starting to scatter with gray. She was clear-eyed, certain of what she was doing. The ceremony took place in the sanctuary of the First Methodist Church, same church that had conducted my father's funeral ten years earlier. A small group of family and close friends attended, and we celebrated, his grown children and us, with a small reception afterwards in the church parlor.

When they left for their honeymoon, Edwin, Ellen, and I followed their decorated Pontiac through downtown. Edwin drove close behind them, honking his horn, Ellen and I yelling out the window. At the city limits, we pulled over, watched them head down Highway 220 and out of our sight, and then we turned around and headed back to our house for a party that lasted well into the night.

He was not my father in any way, nor did he try to be. He had his own complicated history, with five living children and one who had died tragically. He was given to anger, so much that my mother told him she would not tolerate his outbursts, and she insisted on anger management classes before she would marry him. He took them. When he'd feel his anger rising, he'd get in his car and drive until he cooled down. Perhaps not the best strategy for other drivers on the road, but it kept the peace in our house.

He was a college graduate, an engineer. He loved to dance. He used the back seat of his car as a recycling bin, tossing in empty milk jugs until they blocked the back window, and only then he'd haul them to the dump. He treated my mother's grandchildren like his own. He hated Neil Diamond. He made my mother happy, and that's what mattered.

She forgot to tell him that he wasn't supposed to talk about our father. And so, he did. Often. She forgot to tell him not to use the word "Bill," so he did, every time. He told us how much he admired Bill, a real hero of the war, what a fine man he was. He said we'd all been through so much, losing Bill the way we did. I imagined her spilling her heart to Livingston in a way she'd never allowed herself, telling him everything, including that he would never replace the man she lost. I wondered if there were tears, if he held her, let her cry, let her grieve in a way she needed to. I wondered if she told him she'd made a terrible mistake when she silenced us, that she regretted it, that she'd do anything if she could take it back.

I imagined these conversations, this necessary purging so she could move on. I don't know if that happened. What I know is on that day in July, ten years after our father's death, she began her life over again.

I lived with them at our Ridgecrest Road house for a few months after that. I worked for the state arts council, and because my job in Asheboro required a local address, that house and my yellow bedroom was my weeknight residence, but I kept an apartment in Greensboro for weekends. I often felt like a third wheel, didn't like bumping into him in the bathroom we shared, and I began to spend more and more weeknights in the city and not with them.

I was home on a Monday evening in October when Mama called me into her bedroom to zip her dress. They were headed out to dinner with friends, leaving me home alone, which was fine. I had my own problem to stew over. Livingston was in the den, reading the paper, keeping one eye on the TV and the other on his watch.

She was sitting on the pink stool in front of her dressing table mirror. I slipped her dress off the hanger. "What's wrong?" she asked. "You've been moping around the house ever since you got here last night."

"It's nothing," I said to the coat hanger, sliding it back into the closet and draping her dress over the back of a chair.

"No, it's something." She stood and reached for my forehead. "You aren't sick, are you?"

"I'm fine."

"Does it have to do with Dave?"

Yes, it did. It had been two years since Dave and I were together for what some people thought was for life, until I told him I needed a break. I regretted it immediately, but in the split second between my saying it and the exhale that followed, he decided he needed one too.

The two years that followed were restless and lonely. I graduated from college, found summer work in a plastics factory and then a bookstore before starting graduate school and finally landing a writing job. I had a few boyfriends after Dave, but none that interested me. It was not much of a life between work, occasional dating, and a few friends, but it kept me busy. Meanwhile I'd heard from friends that Dave moved back in with his parents in Chapel Hill and started law school. He and I didn't communicate.

In early October, I sent Dave a handwritten invitation to the opening night performance of a play I'd written for the community theater. He surprised me by saying yes. My mother hosted a pre-opening party at her house, which he attended, and we sat together during the performance. He followed me to my apartment in Greensboro afterwards, and we walked to Ham's, a popular university-crowd hangout near campus, a place we'd been a hundred times back when we were together. A couple of hours later, we'd each finished a Philly cheesesteak and a couple of beers, and caught up on the years that had passed, testing these new waters. At least I was. I thought things were going well, and I invited him to stay over at my apartment that night, no strings, just friends. But I imagined us together again, and this time, I wouldn't need a break. That's when he told me his plans.

"He's getting married," I told my mother. I had eased down onto her stool when she got up from it. She stood by the full-length mirror, checking her makeup. She turned.

"Dave is? Oh, honey."

I was trying hard not to cry, and she knew it. She touched my shoulder. She was still in her slip, and the skin of her arm touched my cheek. She didn't say anything for a minute but kissed the top of my head, which was so unlike her that I didn't know what to do or say. We never talked about feelings or anything personal, even since Livingston. Our relationship sat on the surface of both our lives. But here we were, her hand on my shoulder, and both of us committed to whatever was going to be said in this moment.

I didn't say anything. I felt sad for losing Dave and weird because of this conversation. As uncomfortable as I was, I realized something amazing was happening. She was talking to me. Listening. In seconds, we'd risen to a different level in our relationship, and I didn't know if I liked it or not. I wondered if she felt as uncomfortable as I did.

She'd never liked Dave, not in the two years we'd been together. "Cynical," she called him. "I think he's unhappy," she observed. She didn't like that he brought out a *me* she'd never known before, a *me* she was not totally sure about. She pressed on.

"If anybody knows about love, it's me." She reached for her dress and began to step in. While I zipped her up and we smoothed out wrinkles in the fabric, she devised a plan, and I agreed to it: I'd write to him, not once but twice, three times. Maybe it wasn't too late.

If he wasn't interested in me, she surmised, he wouldn't have come to the play. And if he was still interested, he'd write back.

"And if not, it'll be all right," she said, "You can love again."

I wasn't expecting those words, and yet they were so right. I fastened the clasp of her necklace, told her to have a good time, and not to worry about coming home late.

After they left, by myself in the house, I played over and over in my mind what had happened, what she had said, and who she was becoming. She was changing. She was finding happiness. I was the one who couldn't move on.

CHAPTER 17

I heard about Hub Schetters from Enrique Martens, the desk clerk at the Rolduc Abbey in Kerkrade, the Netherlands, who told me he'd be an excellent contact. "And, of course, he has a museum you will want to see," the clerk said. Hub, a local historian with an extensive knowledge of the war and a desire to tell the story, responded immediately to my inquiry. "I'd be honored to take you and your family to important sites in the area. It is too often forgotten."

This morning, we are late arriving at the abbey, a combination of a slow start and unfamiliarity with the geography. The abbey's bell tower etches the skyline, and a stone walkway and heavy wooden doors welcome us inside.

"You must be the Americans," the clerk says. "Your guide is waiting in the library."

"You are Enrique!" I say, reading his name tag. His enthusiastic welcome tells me he is as happy to see us as I am to see him.

A man with an impressive style of thick white hair steps into the lobby. "Barbara?"

"Hub Schetters? I'm so sorry we're late."

"Call me 'Hup,'" he says, sounding the "b" like a "p." It's a phonetic difference not a spelling one, he explains, and we say it back to him in turn: "Hup Hup."

"I don't mind your being late," he continues. "I've been going through documents in the library and planning our day." His smile is quick, and with his ruddy complexion and tall build he strikes me as handsome, strong, and confident. I like him instantly.

Hub spreads a map of the area around a table in the library. We pull chairs close around him and peer over his shoulder.

He is a retired English teacher, he tells us, and for years he worked in the schools. The war has been a part of his life since he was a boy and lived through it. Now he leads tours across Europe—to Normandy, to Mortain, to the sites of the Battle of the Bulge, and more. He talks fast, almost without breathing, and he punctuates every sentence with a smile. He sketches a map of our travel route for today, talks through important stops, including his house where we can see his museum. "Let's go!" he says.

He pulls his gray Toyota ahead of our van, and we follow him out of the abbey towards the village of Kerkrade. We pass over a bridge on a narrow country road and pull into a small gravel lot. The land around us is lush with the new spring foliage. Beneath the bridge, the energetic Würm river flows swiftly, as recent rains have raised water levels almost to the banks. The waters are a vibrant, clear blue, whether a reflection of the perfect sky above it or the absence of mud and silt I don't know.

"This river and the land are the site of one of our most important battles. See that farmhouse over there?" The barn and silo rise from a ragged field of grass. "It was a German headquarters in 1944. American soldiers waded through waist-deep water. They were open targets for German snipers huddled in the farmhouse."

I try to picture this beautiful flow of water with soldiers clambering for their lives, holding rifles in the air or aiming barrels toward the farmhouse. It would have been early October, according to Daddy's journal, a chilly time to be fording a cold river. The ultimate destination was the Siegfried Line on the German border near Aachen. These were intense fighting days, with heavy casualties and only occasional twenty-four-hour rests at the abbey.

"Near here also is where Lt. Col. Paul McCollum was killed. Do you know his story?"

Paul McCollum again. His story threads through our journey alongside our father's. We saw his grave at Henri-Chappelle, I tell Hub, and our father writes of him in his journal. I picture again the young man in a business suit who appears in news clippings in my father's scrapbook and the weary soldier at rest in the grass of Normandy.

"He was picked off by a sniper as he made a lone circuit to check the company's positions on the night after the crossing." Hub walks closer to the bank of the river. "Right about here is where it would have happened."

I watch the water swirl, alive and powerful, between the river's banks. Here is where McCollum's story ended. A few feet from where we stand, across the bridge over the Würm is a dedication to the battle fought at this river ford. The farmhouse once occupied by German troops is visible in the background. Six stone monuments rise from concrete, and on each, in six different languages, including English, are these words: "Beware of those who teach you to hate, for they will not save you."

"Appropriate words for today, too," Ellen says.

Hub nods, studying the passages he must have read hundreds of times. "Our children don't understand what freedom means, how hard it was for us to be controlled by another country. They think freedom is easy. All my life as a teacher, I tried to help them understand this, and I still try. It's the most important thing anyone can know."

He tucks his large hands into his vest pockets and looks toward the river which forms a clear but uneven divide between fields and forest. "It was a terrible thing, this war. We cannot forget it." The silent pose he strikes as he looks to the other side speaks loudly in the quiet of this peaceful spot. Even Edwin is pensive, his chin resting in his hand, watching Hub.

Ellen breaks our meditation. "In our country, most people have no idea what you went through," she says. "Many young people don't even know about the wars."

Hub shakes his head. "It is the same here. Those of us who remember are getting old, and the young don't want to listen."

Here, I think, reminders of the war are everywhere, on beaches and in hedgerows, in bombed-out craters still visible, even in rivers once filled with blood. In America, and especially in the South, we have reminders of the war fought on our land. Battlefields such as Gettysburg, Vicksburg, and Antietam, sprawl across acres in many states, and thousands of people visit them monthly. We collect relics from that war, we dress up as blue or gray soldiers, we fly flags of war as if we're still fighting, we erect statues to remind us of the battles we fought on home soil, another war where, like this one, freedom of an entire population was at stake.

But of the world wars, costing our country hundreds of thousands of lives and changing our country forever, Americans have few physical reminders. A parade every fall, elderly veterans riding in convertibles in their legion post caps, names on family trees of sons or brothers that no one can remember except that they died. Our veterans could have told the story of world war, but so few were willing to talk. Best not to dwell on it, they were told by a society that wanted to move on. And, so, our history books teach us about wars, but they can't teach fear or compassion, loss or freedom. Maybe, I think, the real experience of war can't be taught but only lived. So far, we have met two people—Charles LeBrun and Hub—who lived through the war as children, and their responses are different from the younger enthusiasts—Sabrina, Noël, Vince, and Marcel—whose enthusiasm is contagious but who don't carry the pain of their experience the way Mr. LeBrun and Hub do.

Back in our cars, we pause briefly in the small village of Kerkrade to view a monument featuring the figure of a single American soldier. The monument was erected to commemorate the Old Hickory soldiers that liberated Kerkrade.

"They've been repairing this site for months," Hub says. Metal fencing surrounds the structure, and we can't move close enough to read the small inscription on the plaque. Other barricade materials, orange like ours in America but with words in Dutch, are posted around us. Cracked sidewalks zigzag up and down the street.

Back in the car, a short drive takes us to the neighborhood where Hub lived as a boy. "There's my apartment," he says, pointing to a downstairs stoop in a quiet neighborhood where buildings and small houses line a two-lane street. Today, a few minutes past noon, not much is happening here. An older couple walks, holding hands, on the opposite sidewalk. An occasional car passes.

"Not much change," Hub says and continues. He was six years old in 1940 when German troops invaded the Netherlands and took control of Kerkrade. For four years, he lived under German authority.

"A Nazi woman—a Dutch neighbor who had been a good friend before the war—lived in the apartment above ours. We knew she was reporting people for anti-Nazi activities. People would disappear and not return. We knew they'd been arrested and sent to the work camps. We were deathly afraid of the camps, because the people taken to them never returned. Therefore, we were afraid of the Nazi woman."

As we stroll the sidewalk, I try to imagine myself a six-year-old child, afraid of neighbors, unsure what each day would bring.

"My street, as you can see now, bordered Germany," he continues, "and people across the street from us were Germans."

In 1940, Germans built a barbed wire fence down the middle of this neighborhood street, he tells us. A few years earlier, the Germans and Dutch had crossed that street many times, children to play with other children, young men to court young women, adults to trade recipes and exchange pleasantries. During occupation, interaction of any kind was forbidden. Citizens of Kerkrade knew not to speak across the barbed wire.

Hub pauses, remembering. "Friends became enemies. Everyone was suspicious of everyone. Everyone was afraid. That's why it's so important for the youth to understand what freedom really means."

We stroll down the sidewalk to the corner. I've brought with me a photograph from the scrapbook of a street much like this one showing people carrying suitcases and pulling carts, walking toward the camera and away from their homes. Refugees from somewhere, I wonder, perhaps of Kerkrade, but Hub says no. "Returning to their homes perhaps? There was much celebration when the Americans arrived and drove the Germans back across the border. But these are not happy faces, so I cannot say."

A few blocks down, we stop in front of a beige-front apartment. "My little house," Hub says. His home is a comfortable refuge of antiques blended with colorful modern furniture. Clocks he has collected through the years hang on walls and sit on shelves, including one in an ornately carved German case with a pendulum. His dog, a small terrier, jumps in Ellen's lap. Hub teases Ellen and me, putting his arms around us both for a photo, and he feeds all of us Cokes and vanilla cakes with a light yellow frosting. The large smile never leaves his face.

"Please, come see my museum," Hub says, as we are gathering our bags. He leads us to a small bedroom where his museum, much like Vince's and Marcel's, is on display. Mannequin soldiers and other collectibles of the occupation and liberation of Kerkrade crowd the walls and shelves. He has staged a small scene with a soldier, his rifle, and an assembly of belts, cartridges, caps, clothing, and more. As do our Belgian friends, he cherishes his collection and, most importantly, treasures the stories of soldiers he has pieced together from the equipment and everyday items they left behind. His desire is to break the silences, to bring to life the stories he witnessed firsthand and those he learned after years of study, reaching out to the young and to anyone who will listen.

My father, with a similar desire, also broke a national silence. During a postwar period when soldiers were encouraged to move beyond war, to come home and forget what they'd seen and done and lived or suffered through, he gave words to his experiences— with his army buddies in the neighborhood; with the schoolchildren with whom he shared his artifacts; with his own children, who didn't understand then the importance of listening. Now, though, it is what he left behind—his museum of stuff—that guides us back to those stories.

I think of Uncle Charlie, Daddy's older brother, a sensitive, fun-loving man who enlisted in the US Navy and was on a ship off Utah Beach when the D-Day landing took place. A promising artist and craftsman, Charlie returned from war emotionally shattered, and he would never recover. He talked about the war only when he drank, which he did a lot, reeling with stories of water splashed with blood and bodies, his two children leaning in from their side-by-side couch cushions, learning to love him despite his whiskey and his failures. Men like Charlie suffered without the help they needed. Men like my father were the living salve of a wound that for so many wouldn't heal. If others had listened to Uncle Charlie when he was sober, had asked him questions, encouraged him to keep going, what a different life Charlie might have lived. Might have.

Midafternoon we follow Hub's Toyota back to the monastery. As we pass through the Rolduc Abbey's gate, I picture soldiers shuffling in their tired boots toward the oversized wooden doors, anticipating their next twenty-four hours of clean showers, warm food, and rest. Inside those doors was peace, even if just for a day.

CHAPTER 18

I wasn't feeling well, but I attributed it to pregnancy—my second—and the upset stomach I'd been nursing all day. Saltines were my staple food, and I kept a box in my campus office as well as one in the car. After my last class of the afternoon, I stopped by the bathroom. I'd planned to cut my office hour short and head home before afternoon traffic crowded the highway. My hour-long drive from North Carolina, where my small college was located, to my home in Virginia, included a windy, coastal road with a lengthy drawbridge stop if a boat was moving up or down the Nottaway River.

Blood mixed with water in the toilet bowl, and when I wiped, bright red blood soaked the paper. I felt my face wash out, and I kept one hand on the wall when I made my way down the hallway to my office where I eased into my desk chair, breathing hard. "God, no, no. Please, God." I uttered to myself over and over the chant I hoped would protect me, though it never had before.

Steadying myself so I wouldn't do more harm, I edged down the hall to the nearest office, hoping Andrea, the business education teacher, whose classroom of typewriters was directly across from my office, had not left for home. Her door was cracked. When she saw me push it open, she rose from her chair. "Sit down, Barbara. What's wrong?"

I felt washed out, and my hands tremored. I didn't sit for fear I might bleed on her furniture; instead, I held onto the back of the chair. "I think I'm having a miscarriage." I was sober and calm, being strong, like I'd been taught, but I was so afraid. Nobody had taught me not to be afraid.

Andrea had two grown children. She was a perpetually happy woman who was always smiling; she was not smiling now. She gripped my arm, held onto me as if I might fall. "Let me think," she said. "We've got to get you home." She lived in Sunbury, North Carolina, an hour east, not at all in my direction.

She was practical, steady, and I knew I could count on her. She was the closest thing to Ellen when I needed Ellen's kind of care. Her wheels were spinning, working out a solution. "I'll call Joyce. We were heading home soon anyway." She shared the ride to Sunbury with an English teacher whose office was on the first floor. They'd add an extra hour to their commute to get me home, but I didn't object. My mind was racing beyond her words. I'd had one early miscarriage, so early my doctor thought the positive pregnancy test might have been flawed, but I knew it wasn't. I didn't know much about the biology of pregnancy, but I knew my body. No women in my family—that I knew of, that they'd ever talked about—had experienced one. Ellen gave birth to her first child a year ago with no problems. Surely, it couldn't happen twice, I thought. "Calm down," I told myself. This is normal. "Spotting," it was called, and I'd read about the possibility in books.

"You're probably fine," Andrea said, reinforcing my thoughts, as she set the phone back in the receiver. "You ride with me. Joyce is going to drive your car and follow us to your house." She scooped the handful of papers stacked on her desk and tucked them into a briefcase. "Wait here for Joyce. I'll close your office and grab your purse."

Within a few minutes, I was lying across the back seat of her station wagon, my head against a blanket she kept in her trunk that was now folded against the window. She cranked her engine and waved to Joyce, who'd pulled beside us in my Toyota.

Andrea drove carefully, slowing down for bumps or intersections. "I don't want to shake anything," she called from the front seat. She kept up a constant chatter as we moved along the highway, over the drawbridge, which lucky for us was not up, and across the Virginia line. I didn't know if she meant to calm her nerves or mine with her talking, but it helped us both. Soon we were inching through the afternoon traffic in Suffolk, finally arriving at my house on the other side of town.

I had called Bill from Andrea's office before we left campus, and shortly after we reached the house, he raced in the front door. "The doctor's office said to take you on to the emergency room at Leigh Memorial Hospital. They'll check on you this evening."

I thanked my friends, though in truth I was so caught up in being strong that I don't remember their leaving. Bill and I climbed into the front seat of his car, riding without talking, both of us deep in the uncertainty of this trip and our future, through late afternoon traffic and underground tunnels, into the city of Norfolk and around it on expressways to reach one of Virginia Beach's premier hospitals.

I didn't think I was bleeding profusely, though I was afraid to stop at a bathroom for fear of what I might find. If I didn't look, there'd be nothing to see. My doctor was a fraternity brother of Bill's. He was a kind young man with a wife but no children of his own. He met us shortly after we checked in to the emergency room. After an ultrasound and exam, he delivered the news: "I'm sorry. There's no heartbeat, and the fetus has begun its deterioration." I imagined the edges of the tiny body fading away, dissolving into the uterine fluid like a dollop of butter stirred into a skillet, losing definition.

After the dilation and curettage removed the remains, my tears gushed like the blood had, uncontrollable sobs, soaking the pillow. There was Bill beside me. There was the nurse saying, "It's all right, honey. Just cry it out. You'll have another." But I felt so empty, and the ache in my belly rose up and twisted around my heart. Bill held me, said nothing except, "Are you all right?"

When we arrived home the next morning, I called my mother. "I'm coming to see you," she said, planning a trip for the following weekend. "Would you like that?" I would.

My belly continued to ache from the surgery and my shrinking-back-to-normal uterus. Slowly the physical pain began to ease, though the ache of loss left me numb, immobile. The next day— a Friday—I stayed home from school, but on Monday, I headed down to the college to teach my classes. The news of Andrea's and Joyce's valiant rescue had spread among faculty, and everyone knew about the miscarriage. Some people avoided me, some looked at the ground and said, "I'm sorry for what you've been through."

Faith, a teacher in her early twenties and recently married, wanted all the details, and I found myself glad to give them: the blood, the disintegrating fetus, the dilation and curettage surgery, the shrinking uterus. She listened, fascinated, and it helped me to share my story. Nobody else, not even my mother, had wanted the details. "You'll have another," Faith said, touching my arm. "Just wait. In a month or two, you'll be pregnant again."

As comforting as she meant it to be, it wasn't what I wanted to hear. It was this child I lost, this child who would never ride a tri-cycle or sit in my lap. It was this child who had no name or gender, the child for whom I'd already imagined an entire life.

I didn't know how to grieve, and I didn't know I needed to. I knew how to be strong and not talk about it. I knew how to stuff down the pain and not let others see it. I knew what I needed to do: I wouldn't talk about it. I wouldn't wallow in it. I would go on with my life.

But this loss had knocked me off my feet, ten times ten, so much sometimes I felt I couldn't eat, couldn't sleep, couldn't breathe.

That first week, my mother called every day to check on me. I could tell her how my sore muscles were healing, how my appetite was not great, my energy low. I couldn't tell her that every night I cried by myself, turning my head away from Bill.

Midweek, I asked her, "When you come on Friday, will you bring those photos on my desk in the bedroom?"

She paused. "The ones of me and your daddy?"

There had been two sets of photos taken shortly before he died, both church directory portraits of us in our Sunday clothes, taken in front of a gray backdrop. The first was all of us, Edwin sporting what was left of his Clemson freshman haircut, looking beaten down. Ellen and I were not smiling, and our parents, sitting in front of three glum children, were also glum. It's a family portrait of American gothic, a sixties family portrait, eerie in its lack of joy. I had tucked that one in my drawer. I hated it.

The second set was just my parents in separate photos. My mother looked straight into the camera, her black hair shining, a curl waving down over her forehead. She was wearing a black dress with double-strung pearls, and her face was stern. The slightest upturn of her lip suggested a smile. She was in her early forties and, I thought, beautiful. My father, trim and handsome, wore a suit and tie and, like my mother, looked straight into the camera. He looked much older than he was, his hair thin and gray, his face tired. The photo didn't show the pain in his stomach, but worry was evident on both their faces.

Shortly after his death, my mother first gave the three of us a copy of these photos. I put mine on the desk that I never used in my bedroom, at an angle that wouldn't allow me to see the faces. When I left for college, I left the photos behind. I didn't want them, didn't want to see her not knowing what was about to happen, didn't want his living eyes looking right at me.

"Yes, those," I finally said. I didn't know what drove my desire to see the photos, to have them, to bring him—and, yes, her—closer. I was missing him more than I understood. I was feeling the ache of his death in a new way.

On Friday evening after she and Livingston arrived, she pulled the twin frame from her suitcase. That night, I propped it on my nightstand and studied my parents as if they were people I knew long ago. They were so different from each other, at least it seemed so to me. He was unrefined, uneducated, funny, fun, a veteran. A solid person I expect my grandparents approved of without hesitation. What about her had attracted him? Without him, she was serious and sometimes harsh, a woman with high standards that were sometimes difficult to meet. But together, they made it work as long as they were allowed, and I had both of them in me, of that, I was certain.

When I heard Bill coming down the hallway, when I heard the doorknob turn, I shoved the photos in my nightstand drawer. Even then, I didn't want to be caught missing him.

CHAPTER 19

Our son was born on a snowy New Year's Eve. That spring, my husband, Bill, who was not a farmer at heart or in practice, agreed to till a square of our side yard so I could plant tomatoes, beans, acorn squash, and kale. He knew that for me there would always be another Bill, one who never got angry, never made mistakes, who always loved me, always wanted me to be with him. No living human could measure up to the image of perfection that the fourteen-year-old me had imagined, created, and polished through the years. Now another person, not yet twenty pounds, was demanding his share of me, which I happily gave.

Our Somerset, Kentucky, home was perched on the top of a hill that slanted east toward our neighbor's garage. I sat on the back-porch step, facing the lush square of land that would be my garden, watching Bill in his overalls as he gripped the handles of the rented tiller, turning the ground over and over beneath the tines. In a carrier beside me on the porch, four-month-old Will slept, his belly full of milk. He already sported a full head of light brown hair. His newborn blue eyes were beginning to darken to a deep shade of brown like mine.

The sun's rays moved onto the step beside me, so warm I could see them, so full I could sense a living presence. My father's hand took shape, and I reached out and touched it, feeling his chapped wrists, my hand sliding into his palm as he pressed his shoulder against mine. He was as I remembered him, thin hair spread across his bald head, clear, hazel eyes looking out at the garden where the other Bill sweated and struggled. My father wore the green plaid shirt he always wore on Saturdays when we headed to fishing ponds in the country. Around his wrist was the leather-banded Timex watch I'd kept in my nightstand drawer since 1969. Was it a squirrel nearby, or did I hear his voice, scratching in the light breeze, saying, "Law me."

And just that quickly, as the sun dropped behind the house, the voice, the warmth, and light beside me lifted and was gone.

CHAPTER 20

Eight years later, after a four-year stint living and working in Hazard, Kentucky, Bill, Will, and I lived in Lexington, Kentucky, in a small, rented house. Bill had taken a break from the newspaper business after a successful fifteen-year career and entered graduate school at the university. I taught writing and editing classes at the university and visited public schools in the area as part of the state arts council's artist-in-residence program. Will was a happy, rambunctious child with a creative imagination and a love for his orange cat that would carry through to adulthood.

When we first moved to Kentucky, my Aunt Cola had said, "I hear you're leaving the country." At the time, we laughed at her thought that anything on the other side of the Appalachian Mountains might as well be California. I learned there was more truth to her comment than I could imagine. So far from home, I imagined I could leave behind my weight of grief and start a new life, and for a while, it seemed to be happening. Nobody knew me, nobody knew my story. I loved Kentucky, loved myself in Kentucky. I'd found the seeds of a poet buried inside me, and they were sprouting and beginning to leaf out in words on the page, my eyes focused outward on the vibrant color of the world around me. I'd found a place I felt I belonged.

Monday morning, March 7, that year was cold from snow that had fallen that weekend, but a bold sun was melting what lingered, lending a familiar ambivalence to the day. I was hyperaware of the date, as I always was, but kept it to myself, not speaking it out loud, not even to Bill, and especially not to friends. It would be a day like all the other March 7s that I'd slogged through, and I would, because I knew how, and tomorrow I could move on.

Bill had walked to campus after breakfast. My classes at the community college had been cancelled because of lingering snow and ice on the roads. Will, also home from school, was with his friends Dillon and Ryan in the living room where they'd turned chairs and couches on their sides and covered them with blankets to build a fort. I spent the morning stuffing the Crock-Pot with stew beef and all the ingredients for a soothing dinner. Already the thick scents of broth and onions were stirring in kitchen, and I was tossing clothes into the washing machine situated by the back door. When the phone jingled, I expected Bill to be calling about lunch, and I answered on the second ring.

"Barbara?" the voice said. "It's your mother."

Something is wrong, I thought. Why else would she be calling? Livingston already had survived one heart attack, and he came from a family with cardiovascular issues. Usually, though, she made those hard calls to Ellen, not me.

She was retired now, as was Livingston. They stayed busy traveling, going out with friends, playing a little golf. She'd moved on. Her life was happy, the hardest years long gone. Her call that morning alarmed me. We talked at least once a week, usually on weeekends, and we'd caught up with each other yesterday.

"What are you in the middle of?" she asked in her delicate, soft-pitched voice. "I don't want to bother you." We chatted oddly for a minute or two, and I answered her questions about what the rest of the family was up to, how I was spending my day on household chores and cooking.

Then after a pause, she said, "I just wondered if you know what day it is."

I froze, tensing as though a cramp had seized my gut. I've always known this day, I wanted to tell her, each anniversary spinning and darkening into a shape unlike any other in the year. I'd be all right the next day, but it was something I had to get through by myself. I was used to that. I'd touched the outer layer of my pain with a therapist several years back, but we ended our sessions after Will's birth. I'd moved away from North Carolina where that one day defined me. I'd moved on, I concluded.

"Yes, I know," was all I could say.

There was another pause, and then, as though she'd been practicing, she continued, "It's been twenty-five years. I just wanted to know if you're all right."

It was the question I had wanted her to ask for so long, wanted anybody to ask, but if there was an answer for it, I had buried it deep twenty-five years ago, just like she taught me to. Part of me wanted to take this moment and tell her everything, to let my words spill through the phone line, across the Appalachian Mountains, and into her house. I wanted to open my box and set free my old hurts. Instead, I kept it closed.

"I'm fine," I answered.

She paused, long enough for me to realize this was hard for her too, and maybe for twenty-five years, she'd been wanting to make this call. I pictured Livingston standing beside her, urging her on, maybe even holding the hand that wasn't holding the phone.

"Well, I just wanted to be sure."

Little more needed conversation. A quick change of subject, a few more niceties, and we said goodbye. When I returned the receiver to its cradle, my hand was shaking.

CHAPTER 21

Imagine a cool mid-October day in Belgium, 1944. His helmet sits heavy on his head, but he's used to it by now. A breeze touches the skin exposed at the open collar and sleeves of his uniform. He's survived four months of war, taken care of friends, soldiers, and others who are counting on him to make it through and help them survive. He's done what he could for the wounded, scared, or the ones gone crazy. He's tired of marching, army chow, loss, blood, dirt. He's tired of war. He's tired of knowing somebody's trying to shoot him every day. Today, as he and his buddies head toward Aachen with the order to breach the Siegfried Line and push into Germany, all he wants to do is go home, get a good night's sleep, chow down on some American fried chicken. He can't focus on that, though. What he has to think about is this day, living through it, not getting shot and helping keep his men alive.

He's watching the sky when the red flame whooshes out of nowhere, the mortar round hits the ground in front of him, explodes, shatters, catches fire. Something strikes his arm. He touches his hand, blood pools in his palm.

"We have no record that your father was here," Catharina Scholtens, the abbey's archivist and historian, says. Her light hair and quick smile are welcoming, but there's something in her eyes that makes me think that, to her, we're just another group of tourists. We don't think we are.

I am certain from his journal that our father was in this place because three times he writes that he is. Enrique Martens assured me two years ago that this was the monastery where soldiers rested. I've seen online videos of soldiers playing ping-pong, drinking beer, and laughing together with the abbey's walls in the background. Crackling film footage shows young men in uniform, rested after their time at the abbey, crowding around the gate as they head out in the morning, boasting for the camera, guns over their shoulders. Our father's journal describes rest, hot showers, USO shows, and all the food and beer they could consume, everything offered to the soldiers who arrived at this peaceful place.

Catharina says again when we question her, "No, no, I am certain."

Ellen and Edwin are both sending me glances that say, "What's going on?" I shrug, shake my head.

She smiles, walks a little ahead of us to begin our tour, and glances back when she talks. She doesn't mention him again, and I let it go.

"I'm sure you want to see the chapel first." We follow her down a hallway through a heavy wooden door that opens into the nine-hundred-year-old Romanesque abbey church. It's no surprise that it's cold within the walls, closed to sun as it has been for hundreds of years. The only natural light filters in through the stained glass windows. Columns rise to the ceiling of the multidomed nave, which surrounds us with intricate frescoes in blues, greens, yellows, and reds. Statues, wood pews polished by wear, candles, recessed bays, and more, flanking a hand-hewn wooden floor, lead to a marble altar. I inhale the damp air, ripe with age, mildew, and, perhaps, moldering death; the same air breathed by monks and priests and soldiers if they ventured through those chapel doors in decades and centuries past.

We move to the front of the chapel's altar where two stone tombs protrude a few inches from the floor. The decorative seal covers are flush with the stone, and in the dimly lit chapel, it's hard to decipher the words and images on the decorative tops.

"We think these are the remains of the monk Ailbertus who founded the abbey," Catharina tells us, smiling. "Scholars have argued that it can't possibly be him. Instead, they believe they're the bones of some low-ranking priest or parishioner. Some think it's a woman, nobody knows who, a commoner, though no one can explain how she got here."

We laugh. Catharina is an entertaining guide, and the chapel is full of stories. She tells one more that delights us: St. Norbert was a frequent visitor to the Rolduc Abbey in its early days in the twelfth century. One day he was celebrating mass when a large spider fell into his chalice of already consecrated wine. Even though he expected the spider's poison would kill him immediately, he drank the wine, swallowing the spider along with it. He began to pray. Then his nose began to itch. He sneezed and coughed, and the large spider, intact and very much alive, came out of his nose. It was a miracle!

"Look to your right. Do you see the stained glass at the top of the window?" We have gathered at the front of the chapel now and face the elaborate altar.

A brilliantly colored glass with the image of a black spider dangling from a web above the saint's cup catches the afternoon light.

"It's the spider and the cup?" I ask.

"That stained glass has been in the window for over nine hundred years now."

We laugh heartily and eye the detail of the window, the delicate but delineated legs of the spider, St. Norbert's eyes, turned upward in surprise, and the chalice itself, tipped sideways.

Catharina's stories are fascinating and funny. Even though I'd been hoping to learn more about the soldiers and the war, I could fill in my own details of my father's time here. He probably did not visit the chapel, though I wonder if he and some buddies might have peeked in the door to see what was inside. I doubt he entered a Catholic monastery again during his lifetime. In our part of North Carolina, especially when my father was a boy, protestant churches were planted on every street corner, but few Catholics settled in our small town or in the area. Chances are he had never met a Catholic until he joined the army and found himself serving alongside men wearing crucifixes and carrying rosary beads; their devotional items must have seemed strange to this small town Methodist boy.

Catharina gives us time to walk up and down the aisles, run our palms along the wood pews made soft through use by thousands of worshippers, duck into side spaces with elaborate stained glass and statues, each telling a story. The old chapel is holy, if holy is thick and wooden and comforting. Our voices, even our steps, echo off floors and walls and carry upward to the vaulted ceiling, as I imagine voices and instruments have done for centuries.

We gather beneath St. Norbert, and she leads us from the chapel and the dark, chilled sanctuary down a hallway to the expansive and sunny courtyard, surrounded on three sides by dormitories and on the fourth by the chapel.

"Is this where the soldiers mustered?" I ask. "My father has a picture of troops in formation in a place that seems much like this."

Catharina pauses, and her face looks puzzled, her eyes narrow, as though something has become clear to her. "Your father was a soldier?"

"Yes, of course. An American soldier."

She smiles, takes a deep breath, and shakes her head. "That explains why I couldn't find his name. I thought he was a student in the school. I looked at rolls as far back as we have them, but he wasn't listed. We don't have records of those war years when the school closed and there were no students here. I can't tell you much about his time here for that reason, but I'll tell you what I know."

Something seems to shift in her body language that I can't pin down. She understands what she hadn't understood before: that we aren't simply curious tourists, Americans searching for a vague connection to the abbey, or children of a young Catholic boy. She seems, like many others, suddenly grateful, more attentive, and even her tour shifts to become more personal, citing details of particular interest to us as children of a soldier.

"Yes, these are the same courtyards your father would have seen, though they've been redesigned since then," she begins. Now they sport hexagonal walkways separating the lush gardens of grass instead of the open rectangle shapes of the mid-1940s. A comfortable seating area with tables and chairs is arranged near the door, and already some guests are sipping wine and talking. The dining room is off the courtyard, outside a small restaurant where one can buy a bottle and bring it to a table. It looks inviting. On one side are rooms where hotel guests are now housed. "Most likely your father would have slept in one of those."

Our last stop is the Rococo library, well-known, says Catharina for its collection of manuscripts dating to the abbey's first century. "This room, of course, was strictly off-limits to the soldiers." We linger awhile, attempting to read book titles, running our palms along the smooth, centuries-old tabletops—with Catharina's permission, of course.

In the lobby, Catharina stops at the check-in desk. We've been at this hotel since nine this morning, and it's early evening, yet our suitcases are still in the van. In a few minutes, we'll gather our bags and check in.

"Again, you must forgive me," she says. "We don't have many families of soldiers. In fact, you might be my first tour. I think I have some photos at home if you'd be interested. I can leave them at the desk if I find them. I'll have Enrique make copies you can keep."

Despite her early uncertainty and my doubt, she has given me what I hoped. All our father does in the journal is lead us to the place. She has given life to the name he has written, to his memory here: he's in the dormitory, sleeping in a small bed, sitting at a table with his buddies, buttering potatoes, slicing beef with a knife, maybe sharing a bottle of wine.

CHAPTER 22

Science tells us that motionless water beneath a layer of ice will cool to the temperature of the ice but no more, and the ice will warm to the temperature of the water but no more. However, if water beneath the ice is flowing, as in a stream or creek, the ice will melt. The flow creates warmth. I began to realize that my mother was beginning to flow beneath the years of ice that chilled our relationship. And as she created warmth, the ice that kept me frozen for so many years began to thaw.

She called me every Sunday night, if I didn't call her first.

"Bobbie?" she'd begin in that voice that grew softer but never grew hoarse. "I'm sitting here reading the paper, and I thought I'd check in."

Wouldn't matter if I was in the middle of something, I'd stop, grab a seat, get comfortable. We'd chat, sometimes as long as thirty minutes.

I'm not saying they were intimate conversations, girl talk, sharing secrets kind of thing. Far from it. We talked about what we had for dinner, how she spent her weekend, how Will was doing in school. But we connected. She would never let me get too far away from her voice. She always wanted me to come home.

In truth, I wouldn't let her get too far from me, either, though I'm not sure what drew me back. The minute I'd finish a spring semester, no matter where I was teaching, whether in eastern North

Carolina or the mountains of Kentucky, I'd hit the road for her house, with or without Bill. During cold winter months, at the first sniffle, let alone a measurable fever, I'd be on the phone, telling her I didn't feel good, and she'd lay a cool bath cloth on my forehead through the phone line. Nobody else could do it like she could. She'd wish me a good night, promise to call the next day. The next day she would.

Bill, Will, and I moved with two cats back to North Carolina, though I fought the move, kicking and screaming as we loaded our Ford Escort wagon and drove back over the mountain toward what we used to call home. We bought a house thirty minutes from my mother and Livingston. We visited every holiday, and they'd come up for birthday parties and soccer games or would drop by on their way from somewhere to somewhere. Not much time passed between our visits.

But we never talked about the hard things, not on the phone or in person. We never went back to 1969, and I didn't want to. She lived her life, and I lived mine. When Livingston would mention "Bill," and he often did, I would nod, glance over at my mother, and change the subject. While goodness swirled around me in the shape of a beautiful family, a career with promise, health, and good friends, I could not get beyond the feeling of loss that dogged me, loss I claimed as my descriptor, the card I'd been dealt.

On one blustery January Sunday, Bill kicked the screen porch door of our North Carolina house off its hinges. He was as tense and unnerved as he'd been in months, more. It was enough that our energetic teenage son, out of school for the winter holiday, was bored and demanding rides all over town, and that we'd inherited two Cairn terriers, one black and one blond, from Bill's aging parents. When we had agreed to take them, nobody mentioned they weren't housebroken. We found piles and puddles all over the house, surprises left on carpet patterns, wet spots tracking the hard-wood. It was all we could do to keep up with their messes, let alone the rest of their spoiled-dog needs.

But now, Bill's worst problem since the new year began was a wife sick with something that had confused everyone, including doctors. While keeping up with the unpredictability of a newspaper job and a teenage son, Bill was having to feed me soup and Coke, help me to the bathroom, wake me for medication, and clean the dog poop by himself.

I called my mother. "He can't manage. You know how he is with stress." She had seen his temper rage over a dirty diaper almost thir-teen years earlier and had experienced it a few times since. Though an ordinarily quiet man—his sweetness had won her over when she first met him, and I often joked that she liked him more than she liked me—Bill could blow up suddenly if pushed far enough. It wasn't the first time he'd taken doors off their hinges.

"I'll be there," she said. She stopped by the grocery for milk, cereal, Jolly Ranchers for Will, a couple of frozen pizzas. Bill propped the screen door so she could get in. He was calm and apologetic, as he usually was after a storm. Will skipped down the stairs to say hello and then headed back upstairs where he and his best friend Matt were moving through the levels in Super Mario Brothers.

Two weeks earlier, on New Year's Day morning, after sipping only half a glass of champagne at midnight the night before, I climbed from bed and fell to the floor. Too weak to get myself up, I called for Bill, who was in the kitchen fixing breakfast for Will and Matt. December 31 was Will's fourteenth birthday, and Matt had slept over after the party when all the other boys went home.

"Probably a muscle spasm in your back," the emergency room doctor said. I was given the usual course of painkillers and relaxants and sent home. My symptoms didn't feel like a muscle spasm to me, but I was willing to take any treatment at that point. A fever set in and climbed higher, but I stayed in bed, dopey from the medication and in severe pain despite the muscle relaxants.

That Sunday afternoon, while Livingston sat in the living room, watching sports on TV and napping, my mother pulled a rocker beside my bed. Her reading glasses angled midway down her nose, and she peered over them to see me as I lay propped on pillows. My checkbook was in her lap, and the pen she was using to pay my bills had slipped from her grip. Her fingers—so bent by rheumatoid arthritis and doubly tender today because she'd had to back off on anti-inflammatories which reacted with her lung medicine—must have been screaming with pain, yet she didn't complain.

My arm yelped when I tried to move it. I was groggy from drugs, and my right shoulder was beginning to swell. I struggled to catch my breath, and, slightly feverish, I was sweating through the sheets.

"I can't tell you what's wrong with you," Mama said, "but sweating like you're doing is what the lungs do when they're cleaning out the toxins."

"But mine's a muscle problem not a lung problem," I said.

"We'll see." She folded her hands in her lap. "There's just something odd about it."

She knew about night sweats and toxins. When she was forty-three, the same year our father died, Mama had been diagnosed with bronchiectasis, a chronic lung condition similar to cystic fibrosis. Outside of her college years, she had never been a smoker, though, in addition to living for twenty-two years with a husband who smoked, she had grown up in a house with a father who loved his Camels. "Most likely, this disease will kill you," the doctor had told her then. "It's up to you how long you live."

Twice daily, for thirty years, she "stood on her head," as we children called it, leaning over the side of her high bed, flipping her lungs upside down so they could drain. She'd cough and spit until she could breathe deeply without the rattling in her chest. She was prone to infection and couldn't be around heavy odors like perfume or candle smoke, which set off coughing spells. She would take bronchodilators and use a nebulizer to help keep bronchial tubes clear. Often she needed antibiotics to clear up infections and prednisone to reopen her lungs. In short, she had chosen to live with it, not die of it, for as long as she could.

In bed that afternoon, my body moved without boundary between wakefulness and sleep as she wrote checks, pausing every so often just to relieve her hand and chat for a minute.

Then, something intentional, at least I believed so, happened. She rested the pen in the bend of the checkbook, edged forward in the rocker. Was there a pause before she spoke? A transition between topics? I don't remember the spark of our conversation, only the words, which startled me awake from half sleep.

"You know you left me back then." She looked right at me in a way she hadn't in years, her milky brown eyes zeroed in on mine. I tilted my head upward and listened. She was saying something important, something we'd never talked about. She was talking about those years after my father died. She didn't say his name, but I knew.

"No, you left me." My head lay back on a pillow against the headboard, covers pulled to my waist, although minutes ago, I'd been so warm that I'd thrown them off completely. I was running hot and cold, but the Tylenol had begun to kick in, stabilizing my fever.

She seemed as uncomfortable as I was, but she pressed on. "Well, we're both back now. That's what matters." More words followed, but the minute they were spoken, by her or by me, I lost them. That's how groggy I was, how confused, so much that later I sometimes wondered if we even had this conversation, though I'm certain we did.

Then she leaned over to my bed, her arms open. From my pillow, I reached into her hug, resting my head on her thin shoulder. I could feel her bones against my face. In a moment, we pulled apart.

I wasn't sure what just happened, but I knew it was important. Later that night after she had gone home, tired of lying in bed, tired of the pain and fever, but feeling energized in a different way, as though something had changed, I hauled myself out from under the sheets, struggled into my heavy wool coat and toboggan, and stole out the back door to where my thick-haired dog Langston greeted me on the steps. Half wild, he wasn't allowed in the house. I hadn't seen him in days, and I missed him as much as he missed me. I sat on the top level, put my arm around his warm coat, and said, "I've had the most important conversation of my adult life, but I can barely remember it."

He licked my face, and curled onto the concrete step beside me, and there we sat until Bill stuck his head out the door. "Come on in. You're too sick to be out there."

I wanted to bring it up again with her. I wanted to ask if we'd really had the conversation or if I just dreamed it, and if we did have it, what exactly did we say to each other. I didn't dare. I wanted to call Ellen, but I knew I still couldn't talk about it with her, and, even if I did, she wouldn't have much to say in return. I didn't think about calling Edwin. I barely knew him anymore, and the conversations we did have—rarely on the phone—were stilted and brief. Instead, I recorded the conversation in my notebook, counted it as a gain instead of a loss. Something had lifted, something eased.

The following week, a different doctor diagnosed my problem: a grapefruit-sized lung abscess at the top shoulder-corner of my lung. It had nothing to do with muscles or joints, places they'd been looking.

"Well, I thought it was your lungs all along," Mama said.

The abscess had begun to show itself in a mound on my upper chest. "I've never seen one that size, especially in someone as young as you are," my doctor said. He called in colleagues, excitement grew. I was happy to be his guinea pig and potentially the subject of his journal article, as long as he healed me. He did. He aspirated the abscess, and I began a three-month course of antibiotics. I could breathe again, taking gulps deep into my lungs.

My mother stayed beside me those three months. Her cough increased, her lungs weakened as mine grew stronger. As months passed, she dropped more weight off her already too-thin body. She couldn't stand up straight or for long without coughing. Sometimes I wished I could give her my breath, strong again now. Instead, I wondered if she had given hers to me.

Spring to summer to fall. Outside her pink bedroom window, a purple finch perched on the Hatteras lighthouse feeder, bobbing his head, dipping his beak into Nyjer seeds, occasionally pausing to peer through the glass. Darkness came early these days, and I needed to head home soon to prep for tomorrow's classes and make sure Will finished his homework before dinner. The vegetable soup I had brought for Mama and Livingston was warming on the stove. She was weak but she wore the Calvin Klein jeans she was so proud of, even though she'd lost so much weight she had to cinch them at the waist with a safety pin. Every day she would get out of bed and dress, no matter how she felt. "It makes you feel better," she said. "You're not giving in to it."

The long trail of her oxygen tube snaked through the house from the kitchen on one end to her bedroom on the other, so she could be in any room and still inhale a clear flow of oxygen.

She was sitting in the cane-bottomed chair by the window, beside the candlestand where three matching blue Hemingway books sat between matching bookends. The drapes were still open to the fading light, and she was watching the finch and another finch that had come to the perch beside the first.

I eased onto the blanket chest at the foot of her bed, where she'd told me a hundred times not to sit. I took a deep breath.

"I wanted to tell you something," I began. "The others don't want to tell you, but I think you need to know." I paused, checked to see if she was with me—she was, her foggy brown eyes focused on me now—and continued.

"The doctor says you don't have long to live. A couple of months, maybe."

I paused again. I was trying to stop my voice from shaking, knowing so well that we weren't supposed to talk about hard things. Her gaze on me was fixed and expressionless. It occurred to me later that what I was telling her might have been no surprise. Maybe the surprise was that of all her children, I was the one who was saying it out loud, me, the youngest, the quiet one, the one she once thought had left her.

I said, "I don't know how I'm going to go on without you."

She didn't get up. She didn't say anything. She glanced over at the finches then back at me. I did my best to stay calm, my heart beating too fast to contain it. I wanted to take back my words as soon as I'd said them, but at the same time I was glad I said them. They needed saying. I waited, looked at the floor, at her, at the finches. The pause was forever, the air between us completely still. And then she spoke.

"You just will."

I nodded, taking her words as instructions, as, I was certain, she meant them. She didn't say anything else. She didn't ask questions. I remembered another day, years ago when she told me the same thing she was telling me now: You will get through this. You will move on. You will be strong.

But I would ache deeply without her. I'd shed tears to fill buckets. Despite all we'd been through and all the years I needed her, and she wasn't there, I'd shake my fist at the sky for her too-short run of years. I would say her name over and over.

We sat for a few more minutes, quiet, watching the birds while the sun faded.

"Can you close the curtains?" she said at last.

"Of course," I said. "And then I guess I need to head home." I pulled the cord that drew the heavy drapes across the panes.

"Help me to the kitchen as you go out," she said, reaching for my arm. I held it tight and walked beside her down the long hallway, careful not to tangle our feet in the tubing.

It is possible to love again, she once told me. Love is flexible that way. Like our lungs, it billows and blows, taking in air, letting it out. We breathe in. We breathe out. We breathe in. We just do.

CHAPTER 23

Ellen sat cross-legged on the hard attic floor, sifting through a box of files and loose collections of letters, photographs, concert tickets, and other mementos. Labeled ELLEN, the box had been waiting for her in this space for over twenty years, since she graduated from college, married David, and moved into her own house. An identical box that said BARBARA was stuffed with short stories, college essays, and letters. One marked EDWIN held letters, school projects, the campaign posters for his unsuccessful bid for high school class treasurer.

We found two eras of memories in the attic. The early toys—bears, dolls, games—pushed to the dark corners of the attic belonged to children protected from sadness or harm by doting parents. The later boxes, closer to the attic stairs, held memories from the years after Daddy died, when it seemed the world was out to get us, and no one could save us from that pain. One era gave us fun, happy mementos; the other was filled with sadness. We lingered on the stuffed animals, squeezing them as though we could bring back that innocent feeling of comfort. Boxes of older memories went into car trunks, papers to sift through later, by ourselves. For me, there would be old journals and bad poetry that skirted my true feelings, though occasionally the words described everything I couldn't say out loud. Even writing them back then had felt forbidden.

Plank after plank of dry walnut wood stretched end to end under the boxes. I remembered when Daddy came home and announced, "I bought a tree!" What he bought was rough cut lumber. He'd brought it home with the intention of making furniture with the precious wood. Splintery to the touch, it was a soft, gentle brown. After he died, we laid it out as flooring for the attic. We must have had the most beautiful attic floor of anybody in town.

"Edwin and I were up here last Saturday, just the two of us." Ellen slid her box toward the attic steps so we could carry it down later. Standing wasn't possible with the low ceiling, so she hunched her way to the back where old board games were stacked, and she eased down beside them. "He told me something interesting. I don't know if he mentioned it to you."

No, he didn't, he wouldn't.

"It was out of the blue, you know, the way he is sometimes. He just started talking about Clemson and the year Daddy died."

I stiffened when she said "Daddy." She was looking down, sitting in the shadow of a rafter. My legs dangled over the open attic door. I didn't respond but stopped shuffling papers so I could hear clearly.

"He said he had been so lonely then. He thought we were at home doing fine, but he was down there by himself without anybody to talk to," Ellen said.

"Did you tell him what it was really like here? That we were anything but fine?"

"I did. I told him we thought he was at school having a good time, away from all the horrible stuff here, and he just didn't want to see us. He was surprised, said that wasn't even close to the truth."

As uncomfortable as the conversation was, I wanted to know more. Our parents were gone now, Livingston had moved to a retirement apartment. This house was all we had together, and we were in the slow process of dismantling it, readying it for sale. My mother's dream house, my mother's nightmare house, the house my father barely got to enjoy.

I pictured Edwin a college student, a young man who just lost his father, who was trying his best to make it through the most difficult few months of his life. What nineteen-year-old college friend could share over a beer the weight Edwin was carrying? What friend would be willing to help carry that burden? I'd never thought about what he might have been going through, only, selfishly, that he was not with us.

In the same way we had two sets of memories, we had two families. In the early years, there were three children, sometimes pairing up and leaving the third one out but always getting back together, always taking our positions for photographs, around dinner tables, or on car trips. Edwin was our leader, and we were his troops. When we were older and our parents left Edwin in charge, he'd lay down rules that were stricter than theirs, and he would hold us to them. When he joined us as the third child and not the one in charge, he could lead us into more trouble than Ellen and I could ever dream up on our own.

In the early days, I shared a bedroom with Ellen, which meant sharing closet space, bookshelves, drawers, and giggles sometime late into the night. When finally ready to settle, we would say our prayers after clicking off the lamp. The first to finish tapped the headboard with her knuckles to signal to the other that it was okay to talk. "Knocking on wood," we called it, or sometimes "KOW," for short, one of many secrets that still belongs to just us two.

In the years after, Edwin was gone, and Ellen and I navigated our way through these dark waters in our sad house, welcomed Livingston into the family, and later helped our sick mother live her last days. Edwin's family and his life was in Georgia. His distance felt intentional to me. Even though Ellen was near in proximity, we shared little besides caring for our mother. I followed her to college, and she helped me register for classes and find my way around a large campus. She found comfort with her friends and later a family of her own. Did she share her story of loss with her friends? With her family? I don't know. Did Edwin? I don't know. Bill learned my story in bits and pieces through the years, as I was willing to share it.

Not once did I imagine that my brother might have felt left out, might have needed us as much as we needed him. To me, he was gone. He'd always been gone, it seemed, literally and emotionally. In the last few years when Mama was so sick, he began to make the trip to North Carolina more often, and he never failed to call her on Sunday evenings.

"I get the idea he might want to talk about it," Ellen said.

I tensed. "Talk about what?" I knew.

"You know, Daddy. All that stuff we aren't supposed to talk about."

It had been thirty years, and we'd done exactly as we were told. The rules, even if Mama had broken them with me once or twice, were still in effect, as least as far as we three were concerned. I was excited and interested, but I was also scared. Edwin might want to talk about it, might want to begin some long overdue conversations. Ellen sounded ready. I wasn't sure I was.

"Well, okay," I said. "We'll see."

It didn't come up again until long after our work was finished, long after the house was sold. If our last words about our father had been left for thirty years in the blue bedroom downstairs, our first words back remained in the attic, perhaps rising to the rafters, perhaps being dispersed out the vents by air, or sifting, like fine dust, onto the deep walnut boards we loosened and finally carried downstairs, too beautiful to leave behind.

CHAPTER 24

"I hate Germany," Philippe Krings says, almost as soon as we say hello. His face is stone, his eyes clear and intentional. "Everything —the language, the people, the food, the land. I hate it all."

If we look east, we can see the country he despises so much. A ten-minute walk and we'd be on its soil. That's how close he's lived all his life, yet to cross the Belgium-German border is still for him, sixty-nine years after the war, to enter enemy territory.

We're late arriving, and I apologize profusely, but Philippe seems content with the wait, or else he does not understand my apology. We'd been delayed by concern for Edwin. When he did not come down for breakfast at the abbey this morning, we texted and got no reply. Ellen and I knocked on his room door. He opened it in his pajamas, his glasses still on the nightstand. He didn't know what was wrong, he said. He was just so tired.

"Go without me," he said. "I'll be fine." We didn't argue. If he was sick, he would be better off at the abbey where he could find help he might need. We'd be missing our number one driver, but Bill slid in behind the wheel, I pulled out the maps, and we headed later than planned to Malmedy, Belgium.

At Philippe's suggestion, we have met outside the Baugnez 44 Historical Center in Malmedy, which, according to its website, is a complex, two-story structure dedicated to the Battle of the Bulge and the Malmedy Massacre. I expect a ticket window and perhaps a tour guide, but instead it's a small brick building with only a sign to identify it.

We have pulled in beside a blue Citroën, its door open. Otherwise, the lot is empty. Philippe raises himself out of the car with the help of a cane. "Unfortunately, I see the museum is closed on Monday," he says, turning toward the building. "I am sorry, for though it is small it tells the story of the battle and massacre well, and you would like it."

"It's fine," I say. "We're interested in what you can show us and tell us." Philippe nods, smiles.

I learned of Philippe from Vince Heggen more than a year earlier, and as soon as I contacted him, he responded, delighted to meet us and share his story of the war. Through our brief email correspondence during the winter, I learned that today's guide is seventy-seven years old, has bad knees and feet—"therefore cannot walk well"—and, he told me, his English is very poor. "I'll try to found somebody to help us for translation," he wrote. "Maybe better with the hands!"

Despite the sadness visible on his face and in his eyes, he appears to be a kind man, soft around the middle, with a neatly cut white beard. He's dressed in a white shirt with an open collar and a khaki sport coat, and I wonder if in his younger days, he was a businessman or banker. We struggle to understand his French, and he does only a little better with our English. With luck and patience, and despite our total uncertainty of what he has in mind for us, we plan the day.

This thick growth of evergreens, the Ardennes Forest, rolls like green felt over a lumpy bed. Here in the winter of 1944–45, more than eight-hundred American soldiers lost their lives among the trees. It's easy to understand why our "Battle of the Bulge" is known as "The Battle of the Ardennes" by the Belgians: the woods that dominate the landscape as well as the town itself played a critical role in the fighting. The forest is in the background as we drive west. It seeps between houses like a river moving through a valley, its trees a handsome blue green. In December 1944, these hills were snow-covered, and temperatures dipped below freezing. Now, on this May morning, the forest is rich, healthy, and stunningly beautiful. The lushness is haunting; a thin shroud of fog hovers above the tree line. Skies are a bright blue, cumulus clouds adrift in the azure. How starkly the trees jab the sky. The village, huddled in a valley between the hills, seems at the mercy of the forest, as certainly it was then.

The four of us squeeze into the Citroën with Philippe in the driver's seat. To the left, he points out a field now lush with new grass. This is the actual Baugnez Crossroads where seventy-five American prisoners of war were found buried in a shallow grave, historically known as the Malmedy Massacre.

I first heard about the massacre when I read about it in my father's journal. He wrote:

"Jan. 13 [1945]—Co. moves into attack of Thiermont, Five Points, and Hill 551. Run across appx 75 American POW that had been shot by German S.S. Division. POW were from F.O.B. [Field Artillery Observation Battalion] outfit. All were disarmed and some were medicos. Were covered in about 2 or 3 feet of snow and had been killed for 2 or 3 weeks." I was perplexed by his casual wording, "run across," as though the soldiers had stumbled upon a herd of wild deer in the woods. As horrible as the war was, finding these seventy-five bodies must have been the worst. Did somebody see a hand sticking up out of the snow? A soldier's boot jutting out of the muddy surface? Did the stench of decay reveal their burial site? Did dogs or other animals start digging and find the first body? No history I've read has described the discovery itself, just what was discovered. Maybe, by this point in the war, after so much death, it was just another day, another notation in a journal.

Prior to our trip, I read about the Malmedy Massacre—seeing their fellow soldiers treated so inhumanely was what it took to energize the weary American troops, compelling them to drive harder into Germany and run Hitler out of Belgium.

"It's true," Philippe says. "The massacre, so terrible, was a motivation."

The discovery site now sits solemnly between two buildings—a house and a small cafe. He eases his car to the opposite side of the road where a memorial site erected by citizens of Malmedy pays homage by displaying informational plaques for each individual. Flowers, small Bibles, and other mementos lay at the wall's base, reminding us that these weren't just soldiers, they were sons, brothers, husbands, and fathers. They were seventy-five young men from across the US—a farm boy, a student, a New Yorker, just a bunch of guys thinking about food, mail call, and staying alive. They were boys like our father, who left their cities and their small towns, soldiers who, like him, wanted more than anything to "finish this thing" and get back home. We walk down the path that runs along the wall, stopping to read names and home states. It doesn't feel right to rush, so we take our time and get to know Philippe.

Back in the car, we wind into the forest. Philippe points out locations of important activity or skirmishes as we circle back toward town. Finally, deep in the forest, he begins to tell his story, some of which I've heard before through his emails, but I urge him to please go on.

He was seven and living with his mother and his brother Edgard, age five years, when Malmedy became the center of intense fighting. Malmedy, Belgium, just twelve kilometers from the German border, had been under German control since 1940. French was the traditional language of the small town, but in school under occupation, Philippe and the other students were required to study German. His teacher was a noncommissioned officer in the German army.

The young Philippe refused to learn the language of his occupiers. His mother warned him, "You speak as they ask!" But the seven-year-old refused. Other Belgian neighbors found ways to maintain their separation. Even his mother hated Germans so much that, before occupation when Edgard was born, she gave the baby his name because there was no translation for it in German.

In September 1944, Allied troops liberated Malmedy, and for a brief time, the town once again enjoyed independence. On December 16, German forces, in a final effort to regain control, launched a counteroffensive campaign, taking Allied forces by surprise, and the Battle of the Ardennes began. Allied soldiers were holed up in the woods, with temperatures remaining below zero degrees for days, snow continuing to fall until it reached a height of thirty inches.

Meanwhile, Philippe's mother—his father had died of typhus in 1943—accepted the offer to host a dozen American GIs in her home.

"We provided them with a shelter, a family, warmth, clean laundry, and a little heat," Philippe tells us. "Their youth made us feel safe . . . and the K rations, the chocolate, and the Nescafe were more than welcome." He smiles slightly, a glimpse of teeth between his beard and mustache. One soldier gave young Philippe the olive-colored plastic liner of his helmet, which the boy wore with delight. Inside the helmet, in red paint, the soldier had written his name: Joseph Corbeau.

Bombing by German and American forces continued. On December 23, the town itself was besieged by fighting on both sides, and civilians as well as soldiers were injured and killed. "A bomb fell thirty feet in front of the house, another one at the back, just a little farther. Doors and windows were destroyed but we were safe!"

His mother, though, fearing for their safety, sent the two boys to their grandmother's house a few blocks away where a dozen people were already sheltered in the basement.

"On December 24, that afternoon around two-thirty, there was another air raid, and the town was targeted," Philippe continues. "The house was hit by a direct blow and the two floors crumbled down onto the cellar where we were gathered."

American soldiers rushed in immediately, first using bulldozers and then their hands, digging through the rubble until they found the boys. Philippe was badly injured. Edgard's skull was crushed.

Sgt. Joseph Corbeau and another soldier put both boys in a Willys Jeep and drove to the US military hospital in Eupen, twenty miles away. To get there, they had to breach the German line and barely escaped capture, saved most likely by the chaos that was everywhere on that day. Doctors successfully treated Philippe's injuries. Edgard died that day. Almost the whole city was either destroyed or burned.

Our father's journal tells a soldier's side of the battle of Malmedy. On December 23, the company set up positions to defend the town from further attacks. German paratroopers in American uniforms dropped in at night to sabotage the rear. Bombing by both sides was relentless, and the people of Malmedy, caught in the middle, suffered severe damage, from the loss of human lives to the destruction of the entire village.

On December 24, 1944, my father wrote, "Town again bombed by American B-26 or A-20. Town now in ruins and burning. Casualties very heavy." The journal describes the day after as a much quieter scene: "Company enjoys Xmas dinner at supper time. Roast turkey with all trimmings. Red Cross stockings received by all men containing socks, candy apples, oranges, and nuts. All men gave stockings to kids of Malmedy whose families had been killed in bombing."

"Yes, this is true," Philippe remembers when we tell him of the journal entry. "Many children received American stockings. Many citizens, including children, had died."

After the war, Philippe grew up, married, had children of his own, and enjoyed a successful career. Years passed. The story of the American soldiers who saved him and tried in vain to save his brother stayed with him. Several years ago, he remembered the plastic helmet liner and his rescuer's name painted in red. He remembered that Joseph Corbeau had been a member of the 30th Infantry Division, 120th Regiment.

Philippe began a search, first by mailing letters to American strangers named Corbeau and eventually on the Internet where he found his soldier. Sergeant Corbeau, born in 1913 in Cumberland, Maine, returned there after the war and spent his life in his home state until he died in 1994 at age eighty-one. Philippe was never able to thank Sgt. Corbeau in person. Nor has he been able to find the names of other soldiers who stayed in his mother's house.

"I have been terribly marked by this incident," he tells us. Even as he speaks, so many years later, his eyes grow dark. His hatred of Germans is raw, but on this afternoon as he retells his story, I can't stop from thinking: because the American forces were responsible for most of the bombing of Malmedy in their attempts to drive the Germans out, Philippe and Edgard were likely hit by American, not German, bombs.

Back home, before our travel began, I'd located records of a telephone conversation on December 25, 1944, between Major General Leland S. Hobbs, commander of the 30th Infantry Division, and Col. Raymond Hill in which they describe unsuccessful attempts to evacuate ten thousand citizens of Malmedy. Evacuation incomplete, the air raids escalated in order to root out the German troops, and according to Hobbs, "Our own bombers bombed the hell out of Malmedy yesterday." He concluded, "Citizen casualties are severe."

Why then did Philippe not hate Americans too?

I should ask, but I don't. Whatever his reasons, in Philippe's story, Americans are the heroes, and forgiving Germans is simply not an option. That fact I clearly understand.

We pause in our visit to "take a drink" with Philippe at a side café in Malmedy, a small but welcoming town of eleven thousand. We gather around an outside table, drinking stouts and munching sandwiches. A group of students sits at the table beside us, smoking, talking, and enjoying the warm midday sun.

Philippe glances at the youth, turns back to us, and grips his hand around the handle of his mug. "They don't understand," he says. "Young people laugh and have a good life, and they don't know what we had to endure for them to be free. They don't care to listen. They don't want to know." There's anger behind his words, visible in the deep lines of his face.

"Do they study the war in school?" Ellen asks.

"Not much. Our story is here, all around them, but they won't look, won't see." Again, Philippe's face tightens.

"It's the same in our country," Ellen replies. "Our daddy would talk about it and bore us to death. We didn't care about it until we grew old enough to appreciate it, and then we didn't have him to ask anymore. Maybe one day they'll want to know, just like we did."

Philippe shrugs. "We must hope."

After lunch, we follow him down Malmedy's main street sidewalk along a mix of new establishments and older structures to the town square. Bombing destroyed most of the historic architecture, as my father's journal describes and Philippe confirms, but a tenth-century cathedral sits prominently at the top of the grassy mound, its ancient spires rising.

"Our Cathédrale Saint Pierre miraculously was untouched," says Philippe as he climbs the stairs to the heavy doors, propped open for visitors. Philippe tells us that the cathedral, originally a Benedictine abbey, was burnt down during the French Revolution, but has been in place since its rebuilding in the late 1700s. It's a massive building, gray and uninviting from the outside, but inside, its stunning elegance is breathtaking. We step into the vestibule that welcomes us into a large sanctuary with two rows of wood pews. Light transmits dimly through the many stained glass depictions of biblical stories. A quick glance reveals angels, lambs, John the Baptist, and more both recognizable and obscure figures from the Old and New Testaments. Scattered along the wooden altar, a dozen votive candles flicker, each one a prayer left by a visitor for a loved one. A man sits alone in a pew, his head bowed; another small group of visitors lingers along one side, pausing to view the gold molding and the larger-than-life statues. We speak in whispers to honor the silence, snapping a few photographs but no more because even the small camera click interrupts the quiet.

"I'm so glad it was spared," I say. That it avoided major damage is remarkable, almost impossible to imagine amid the ruin of this town as Philippe has described it.

I fold my arms for warmth. The sun outside is strong, but inside this cathedral, just as in the Rolduc Abbey's chapel, the air is cold, damp, and ancient. Except for a few who are lingering, visitors don't stay long. We walk up and down the aisles, stopping to note architectural details cunningly devised or stained glass images. I imagine war raging outside this place, bombs falling on its steps, perhaps aimed for its steeple, the wind blowing mortar rounds off target.

Back outside, Philippe stops at a stone wall. "Here we have erected a memorial for our soldiers killed in the bombing." Row after row of company names. "These are units who fought here. See your father's is listed." I bend to see the lettering to which he refers: "30th Infantry Division" is scripted in gold on a dark plate.

Behind the cathedral, a small quadrangle-shaped yard is set apart from the busyness of the streets. A group of young men lounges in the grass, stretched with their arms beneath their heads or sitting, legs crossed, and chatting. Others stroll the sidewalk. A couple holds hands while children play nearby. We follow Philippe to the far end of the yard where a concrete slab etched with names rises out of the ground toward the sky.

"These are the hundreds of civilians killed in that two-day period," he explains. He points to the top and to one name:

Krings, Edgard, 5

The name leaps off the wall as though emblazoned in silver. "My brother." He traces his finger along the letters spelling out his brother's name. I imagine he has done this many, many times.

We linger at the site, first allowing Philippe time for the reflection that he seems to want. "I don't come here much anymore," he says. "Only when there is a visitor or sometimes when I want to remember."

We wait quietly, walking along the curving sidewalk. Beyond the wall of names, four young men with two cameras on tripods stroll back and forth across the sidewalk, as though they are waiting for someone or trying to decide what to do next. The one who seems to be in charge notices us, comes near. His hair is close-cropped but unkempt, as though it hasn't been combed for days.

"Are you a family member of one of the deceased?" he asks in English.

"Excuse me?" says Ellen.

"The wall. Do you know someone?"

We repeat the history of Philippe and his brother.

"And what about you?" he asks. "You are Americans, yes?"

We tell him of our journey from Omaha Beach to the Elbe River following our father's map across Europe. He listens carefully, leaning in, and nods his head.

"We're making a film about the journey of the soldiers through Europe during that time," he says. "May we interview you?"

He calls in French to the two cameramen resting in the grass. They lift themselves up on their elbows. "Oui, oui," I hear, as they rise. Ellen and I stand side by side in front of the wall of names, the French director begins his interview, and the camera rolls. He wants our story, and so we tell it, answering his questions as we are asked, responses alternating between us.

"Come, Mr. Krings," Ellen urges. "He would love to talk with you too."

"No, no," Philippe responds, and moves to the edge of the lawn to wait with David and Bill. He is restless when we rejoin the group, perhaps concerned that we've told too much.

"I'm sorry to slow us down," I say.

"You must tell your story. That is what they want to hear," he says. I recall our lunch conversation and his reproach of the young, and wonder why, now that he has an opportunity to reach a wider audience, he backs away. There's a sadness in his face that wasn't there before. We have stirred up old emotions and memories with our visit today, and while he has given willingly, I wonder how difficult it is for him to relive that time.

When we left the Rolduc Abbey this morning, we promised David we would make a side trip to Bastogne. "That's where a lot of the Battle of the Bulge took place," he said. "They've just opened a new museum."

We explain to Philippe the best we can that there is another side to this battle we must study, the other major conflict in the Battle of the Bulge that raged fifty miles to the west while bombs dropped on Malmedy.

"There is never enough time to learn about war," he says, regret in his face.

"We'll come back," I say, and mean it, though I also remember that he is seventy-seven years old, and he has given us perhaps the best day we could have hoped for.

We make one more stop before driving south to Bastogne. His grandmother's house is a modest two-story brick structure with a bay window which stands at the corner of a busy intersection. He pauses on the curb, his engine idling. We don't get out of the car— Philippe is not sure who lives in the house now or if they would appreciate our poking around. I sense he has done this many times. He points to the lowest windows. "There, in the cellar, is where we were."

I can picture the two small boys, huddling with others in the cellar, afraid, while bombs scream through the night, their cries when one comes close, their screams when it hits.

We linger on the curb for a few moments until Philippe eases away from the curb and drives back to the museum where we left our van.

As we are saying our goodbyes, Ellen pulls a photograph from her purse. "I wanted to ask you about these girls." The picture is from the scrapbook. Our father, in helmet and heavy wool army jacket, is standing in front of a deep snowdrift beside a set of stairs, his arms around two young girls, one blond and one brown-haired. They might be eight or ten years old.

"They look like us," Ellen said when she first saw the photograph over a year ago. He's smiling at the camera, his hands cupped around their shoulders. I, too, have studied the photo, the faces of the little girls, and our young father, who, when the photo was snapped, might have been thinking of his own future and daughters he might have.

"No, I don't know them. They would have been a year or so older than me." I've made an extra copy of the photograph, which I offer to him.

"Will you ask around? Maybe someone will recognize them,"

Ellen asks. He slides the photo from my fingers, studies it, and then tucks it into his coat pocket.

Saying goodbye is difficult. Despite the long life that Philippe has lived after the war, he carries his grief from so many years ago as though it were yesterday's sorrow. So far on our journey, we've met with gratitude and sadness, but this is something different. The experience has shaded his eyes, diminished his smile, coursed throughout his body, even to his knee, which hurts with each step. Is this what old grief looks like? I wonder. Is this tomorrow's image of me?

I think about Philippe, his grief for his brother Edgard still so raw, his wound open. I think about pain and anger, blame and for-giveness, about years that pass by quick as a heartbeat and slow as a sleepless night. I think about hurt so deep it feels as though life can't go on.

Then I think about going on.

CHAPTER 25

Bastogne is a wild goose chase across the Belgian countryside. I drive, Bill navigates, Ellen and David sit in the back. It's a long trip in the opposite direction from the Rolduc Abbey. It's getting late. We're tired. We're driving further away, and we're looking at a two-hour drive back to our rooms.

The museum is closed. As with the Baugnez museum, Monday is its day off. We climb the steps to the circular concrete memorial, study the wall charts and plaques that hang on its interior walls, and then clamber back in the van and head to the abbey, frustrated and in dire need of rest. Even though it's what I feel, I stop short of saying, "I told you we should have stayed in Malmedy." Being right is a hollow victory, and I keep it to myself.

Two hours later, we park and walk across the abbey's parking lot like weary pilgrims, shuffling through the doors and down the hallway toward the dining hall. We're about to turn onto the staircase when Ellen says, "There's Edwin."

He sits in the courtyard, leaning back in a metal chair, a bottle of red wine on the table, a glass in his hand, a new friend at his table. Our brother looks renewed, a fresh recruit. When he sees us, he waves. "Come join us!" he calls.

Not one of us feels like socializing. We're hot, tired, ready for a nap, but we step into the courtyard.

"Feeling good," he says when we ask. "Extra sleep this morning, a long, hot shower, and lunch. I'm good as new." Perhaps Edwin had it right all along. Perhaps this old monastery is giving him exactly what he needs, what we all need—rest.

That night when we meet in the Rolduc dining hall, set up for fine dining, I'm refreshed—showered and in clean clothes, content with our success on the trip so far, and relieved that my brother is on the mend.

We finish several bottles of wine among us. We eat delicious servings of salmon and chicken breasts, prepared by chefs who come out to shake our hands. We recall with much laughter Catharina's story of Ailbertus's missing sarcophagus and the mystery woman taking his place in the crypt, and our joy bursts uncontrollably when we remember St. Norbert who swallowed the spider that then came out his nose. After our dishes are cleared from the table, I look around. We've been wined and fed. It's the kind of giddiness I remember from early childhood, three children who can't stop giggling in spite of their parents' warning, until finally the parents join in. David and Bill are laughing too. Here we are, I think, in a monastery in the Netherlands, rediscovering one another. Not just any monastery, but our father's monastery, where he must have sat, in this dining room, showered, rested, enjoying a pint of beer.

It's an overwhelming feeling of both accomplishment and awe. Whatever we are on the trail of, we are coming closer to finding it. I can't put words to what we are seeking. It's as if we are following a treasure map not knowing what's buried beneath the X.

The next morning, when I look out the window of our small room at the Rolduc Abbey, I see the N299 highway, which we'll take today. The long driveway winding away from the doors of the abbey to the main highway is a slow return to a busy world, and for us as well as the soldiers, the rest of the war. I cherish what I've gained here, a reminder to slow down and accept the spirit of the place as its gift to us. Fat-bellied goats grazing on the hill above don't look up. These are working goats, Hub Schetters told us, hired by the city as bovid lawn crews to keep grass trim and neat. It's another day, the goats seem to be saying, and grass is abundant.

In the dining hall, now set for breakfast, a bountiful spread of food stretches across several tables—ham slices and sausages, cheeses, eggs, cut and whole bananas, apples, pineapple chunks, croissants and breads of all kinds, jelly, peanut butter, chocolate, two kinds of coffee, orange, cranberry, and grapefruit juice. I fill my plate twice, even sneak boxes of chocolates into my pocket for later.

We have the entire day to drive north across the border, and make our way to Duisburg, Germany—a short, easy trip. After breakfast, we take advantage of a late checkout time and don't hurry to leave. David explores the area surrounding the abbey, hiking across the border to Germany and back. Ellen rests her sore knee. Edwin lingers in the dining hall; he's found someone new to talk to. Bill and I walk along the fence of the small farm adjacent to the abbey, around the pond and to the menagerie of sheep and goats, llamas, ducks, and pigs. Even the timid deer come to the fence in greeting.

I know for certain there is a healing spirit in this old monastery. When we arrived, we were weary foot soldiers in dire need of rest. These walls have held us in their arms as we've slept, eaten, rested, and most of all, laughed, as we always did as children. There is healing in laughter, and there is love. What magic here that strengthened the soldiers has strengthened us. Yet, our journey—like the soldiers' when they paused at the abbey—is not yet done.

When we stop at the desk to turn in keys, there waiting is a bottle of Rolduc Abbey wine, left by Catharina Scholtens from her private collection.

"To the Presnell family," reads a note taped to the label. I tuck it in with Edwin's souvenirs, to be savored later.

As we pass through the abbey's doors, I remember the news reel of American soldiers taken at the Rolduc Abbey after a night of rest and recuperation, their unbuckled helmets sitting on their heads like loose bowls, their foreheads exposed, freshly shaved faces as innocent as boys playing army in a backyard. They are ready for more, those faces say.

CHAPTER 26

Last night's shower soaked the low-lying roads that led to the St. Bernard Parish Cemetery in southeast New Orleans. I drove our rental car from a housing work site on a street called Tiffany Court, circled through neighborhoods abandoned or in repair, paused by an overgrown marsh to watch a white heron ankle deep in water, and finally turned into the quiet lot of the cemetery. I was burdened by a mood I couldn't shake: something was off, but I couldn't put my finger on what. The heavy iron gate of the cemetery shined in the rain. Perched on its brick post was a marble angel with her head bent back, trumpeting into the muted sky. My cell phone buzzed, and my brother's name popped onto the screen.

"I was playing with my phone," Edwin said when I answered. "I wanted to see if I could get you and Ellen on a conference call."

"Sure." I cut the engine. "Go ahead."

I was here in St. Bernard Parish with a group of twelve college students, one other faculty member, and Bill, all of us volunteers in the Alternative Spring Break program sponsored by Habitat for Humanity, building houses to replace those washed out in the floods following Hurricane Katrina. We worked all day and then spent our nights in an elementary school building used as temporary housing for volunteers, a place now called Camp Hope. Rain had poured down almost every day, mocking our generous spirits and slowing our work. Every night, we headed into the French Quarter, alive with music, tourists, beads tossed from balconies, and air mingled with the scent of smoke and beer. Students needed the fun after working all day, we three advisors said. In truth, we loved the nights as much as they did, strolling down Bourbon Street smoking cigars, stopping for beers, looking the other way when our underage students flashed their fake ids.

Edwin put me on hold while he tried to reach Ellen. I watched the rain pirouette down my windshield, tightened my jacket around my neck. The paths of the St. Bernard Parish Catholic Cemetery were puddled with water.

In a few minutes, he was back. "She's not answering. But I've got her voicemail, so we can leave her a message."

He spoke first, explaining to our sister the missed opportunity to talk to both of us at the same time. Then me: "Hey, Ellen. I'm in New Orleans, building houses. I'm sorry we missed you."

"Okay, that's it," Edwin said. "I've got a lunch meeting, need to go. Are you all right?"

"Tired, smelly, sleepy, and ready to come home. Otherwise, I'm fine."

"I mean . . . ." His hesitation on the other end made me pause. I'd lost track of days. Today was March 7. No wonder my funk, no wonder Edwin's out-of-the-blue call. This day had haunted me—haunted the three of us—for thirty-nine years, still barely a word spoken about it. If the weight of the day was why Edwin was reaching out, I couldn't imagine what he wanted to say. It's a day that had always stopped me, a date I could never skim over, a day tattooed on my bones.

After dinner, I waited in the Camp Hope community room line to check my email. Half a dozen computers were arranged against the beige wall where two soft couches, a few tables for board games, and a TV mounted in a corner provided the best hangout space among buildings on the school grounds. A small crowd had gathered, college students trying to relieve stress after working all day in the rain on various sites.

When my turn came at a computer, I logged on and typed in my password to retrieve incoming mail. There was only one, from my brother, sent to both Ellen and me. The subject line was blank. I double-clicked, and the message opened. "Dear Sisters," Edwin wrote, "I tried to get the three of us on a three-way call today because I was in a deep moment of reflection. Every year since 1969, I and presumably you, relive at some point the biggest turning point of our lives. Since then, of course, other days bring about similar emotions . . . but the events of 1969 cannot escape me as the single most defining moment of my entire life."

As I focused on his words, the rest of the room fell away. My pulse began to race. I wasn't sure I was ready to get into what I feared was coming—a retelling of the past, something he had never shared, and I had only touched on with Ellen in an attic years ago. We don't talk about this, I wanted to remind him.

I read quickly, hungrily, then doubled back and read again. He detailed the days of March 6th and 7th, 1969, of the early morning phone call from Mama to the hallway phone in his dorm, his hitchhike home that took most of the day, of not knowing what he'd find when he arrived. He described being at the hospital with Mama during that long night and into the morning. I could picture him there by the bed, standing beside his father, the tubes carrying oxygen and fluids and machines recording worsening numbers. And then he wrote, "I can see to this very day and I see it more frequently, less than an hour before the end, the faint smile of encouragement and approval combined with a feeble grip of my hand."

Edwin had been allowed—he'd been expected—to stay at the hospital with our mother. I had wanted to be there, but Ellen and I were sent home to bed. Not only was Edwin there on our father's last night, but he got from him a signal, a smile, a squeeze of the hand. I should have been happy for Edwin, but what I felt was envy, maybe anger, and certainly unfairness. I didn't get anything, and certainly not a hand squeeze or smile. What a difference it might have made, I thought, to have had a final message, something I could hang on to through the years, even just an acknowledgement that I was there. In my last visit on the day before he died, he was unconscious, unresponsive.

I swallowed down my envy to accept the magnitude of this moment. Edwin had broken the wall of silence. His story was remarkable to me because I'd never heard it. It was perhaps more remarkable that I'd never heard it in the almost forty years that had passed. At last, he had defied our mother's mandate by saying forbidden words and beginning a conversation I wish we'd started that night in the dim light of Ellen's bedroom. Instead, that door to our honest futures closed, and no one, not even our mother, had a clue of what that closing was going to mean or how long that door would be locked. It had taken thirty-nine years, but my brother, my brave, courageous brother, had stood up and said, "It's been long enough."

I sat at the computer, reading his email over and over. I couldn't take it with me because there was no printer. I tried to memorize what I could. People around me came and went. Users logged on, logged off, and still, I sat until I heard a familiar voice.

"Barb, you all right?" Bill stuck his head in the door. "I'm going to bed. Come on. It's late. We have an early day tomorrow."

I logged off and shut down the computer. Later, as I lay in my bunk for the last night in the temporary dormitory, images swirled: the hospital room, my father, pale and near lifeless in a thin hospital gown. His hands, rough with eczema, dangling outside the sheet but strengthening to squeeze my brother's hand. His green eyes, opening for a blink, long enough to see my brother, long enough for my brother to see him back.

The next day, we boarded our plane in Biloxi, Mississippi, glad to be heading home. Ellen met Bill and me at the airport in

Greensboro. Rain still teased around the edges of morning, a soft pattering on her windshield. After a quick rundown of trip details, I asked, "So, did you read Edwin's email?"

"I did." We were pulling into her driveway, late afternoon's overhang of winter chilling the March afternoon.

"So, what's going on with him?" I asked. "And what are you going to do?"

"You know he's always a wreck on March 7," she said. Did she know I was too? "I'll answer, but I need to think about it first." As was her habit, she would weigh all sides, check the highs and lows of everyone's temperatures, and then find her voice.

Bill and I were home before dark, and after I unpacked my suitcase and loaded the washing machine, I sat at my computer and reread my brother's words, the tender story of a boy turned man in a single weekend.

After a while, I began typing: "What I remember is the vomiting."

In the long email that followed, I told my version of that day, that year, and the years that followed. To my surprise, words gushed from my fingers onto the screen. I recalled the day of our father's death, of Mullie Chandler waking Ellen and me before daylight, that day beginning in clouds, how those clouds hung around all weekend until I began to think there would always be rain. I told of the long grief that followed for all the years he was gone. "Had he lived 39 more years—or even 29 or even 19," I wrote, "how very different our lives would have been." For an hour or more, I was back in a time I rarely allowed myself to relive, and being there was easier than I expected. Telling the story felt good, and I felt different just reading over my words, as though I was sloughing off layers of extra skin. I hit "send" then closed my screen and stood, stretching my arms behind my back. I was spilling words I'd never shared with anyone. Bill had heard most of my story through the years, but he didn't know the detail or the emotion that grew from those details. That evening, I shared with him Edwin's story and more of my own that he didn't know. He listened closely, and my grief seemed to loosen its hold even more. That night, I went to bed exhausted, relieved, and strangely happy.

Ellen's reply didn't come until Tuesday, two days after our return from New Orleans. It was a damp morning, and I'd developed a slight cough since our Habitat trip, due perhaps to the weather or perhaps to the FEMA trailer where we spent most of our downtime on the work site. Bill had it too.

Tuesday was a teaching day, so I was scrambling to make lunch and hit the road. I was running late, partly because of the cough and partly because, even though I was coming off a break, I was far from rested.

I grabbed two slices from a loaf of bread, laying them like mirror images on a paper towel. If I hurried, I could still be on time for my eleven o'clock class. My laptop sat open on the counter beside me, and I tapped "Get messages," in case there were student emergencies or panic over assignments. A dozen emails popped onto the screen, but only one mattered, from Ellen. I hoped it was her response, but, like Edwin's, the subject line was blank. I'd take only a quick glance, I told myself, then I'd come back to it when I had time to linger. I clicked it open. The message scrolled down the page. She wrote: "I remember like it was yesterday that I got on my knees at my bedside and started praying. I prayed to God to heal my Daddy and make him well, and for us to be able to accept whatever happened. I remember CLEARLY being overcome with a sense of calm and assurance that he would, indeed, be healed and that we would be ok. Somehow, I knew he wasn't going to live, but he would certainly be healed."

She had been treasurer of our church's Methodist Youth Fellowship that year, and the group hosted a hot dog supper a week or so before that had been lucrative. Our father, she remembered, helped her count and recount the proceeds, helped her write out the deposit slip for the bank, and promised to take it there before he checked in to the hospital that Monday for surgery.

"Don't get the idea that the sense of calm I had that night was enough for me to get through it," she continued. "By no means. What it did was make me aware of a greater power that really was in control, whether I liked it or not."

Of course, she had not shared with me her prayer, the response to her prayer, or her resulting calm. Neither had I shared with her then or in my later years my nightly journal writing, playing albums on the record player in my bedroom, or lying on the floor by my bed, my door closed.

"Afterward, we just lived in total sadness."

Separately and alone, I wanted to add. Silent.

"Now, how has it all affected me and the ensuing years of my life? First, I learned that I would have to depend only on myself."

In those years after, we did our own plumbing, cleaned our own gutters, wired our own lamps. Three women, in charge, yet falling apart. She turned to her friends, made a new family, found a way to recover some of what she'd lost.

"Second, I know that we have no control over things that happen —good or bad."

Growing up, I wore her hand-me-downs—her Easter dresses and school skirts and the dungarees that were passed down to her by our friend Lee. Our Aunt Peggy would sew us matching outfits— red jumpers with white blouses, crinoline-skirted Sunday dresses, lightweight jackets. I'd wear each one twice, first until I outgrew my own, and again until I outgrew Ellen's.

Ellen's hair was blond and mine was brown, but we wore it the same—shoulder length or shorter, bangs to our eyes, a flip of curl at chin length. We sat side by side for perms together. We visited the dermatologist together. We shared dental appointments, doctors, teachers. For many years, people would say, "Now, which is Ellen, and which is Barbara?" For all those years, we were who our parents made us to be, alike on the outside, but different on the inside. We were the same height, but she towered over me in goodness, style, and most everything else. She watched over me.

Until the day our family shattered. Something changed between us then.

"Third, I have learned the true value of friends."

We spent time together, but we didn't talk about what mattered. She turned to friends and, later, her husband David and the new family she married into.

In the library during high school English class when we were supposed to be doing research, I sat in a private carrel and listened to Simon and Garfunkel sing, "I Am a Rock." Mrs. Snyder, my English teacher, left me alone. She knew I was "troubled," and I suspect she knew why, though she never brought it up. She knew I could write an A paper, and she must have assumed that music and privacy were much more important to me than English class. I watched the hands on the round clock in front of me to know when it was time to lift the arm of the record player, turn the album in at the checkout desk, and head off to lunch—"And a rock feels no pain. And an island never cries"—where I met my so-called friends who had no clue how lonely I was.

One Friday night, my mother reminded me I had no friends because if I did I'd have plans to do something with them, go to a movie, or head over to somebody's house. "I do too have friends," I said and stormed to my room where I picked up my journal and started listing people I called my friends. Anyone who might like me. I counted six, but I set it aside, certain I would come up with more.

Ellen would have been at Debra's house that Friday night, and Carey was probably there and Cathy, Bill, and Jim, and I didn't even know who all her friends were. Church friends. More than anything, I wanted to leave here, this house, this town. Get me out, I thought, and I will show you how much people will like me.

"Fourth," Ellen continued, "I learned to try to love every minute of my life because I know that it can be cut short in a minute.

My sister. So happy. So pleasant. Impossible to ruffle, no matter how much Edwin and I would try. But she always stayed so busy: career, graduate school, two young children. Scouts, 4-H, trips to the beach, church, friends. Stillness was hard to find, to the extent that often I wondered if she avoided it. She wore a protective shield of God and friends, and I wasn't part of it.

"Even with the sadness we have experienced in our lives, we are all still blessed beyond measure. I am so thankful for what they instilled in me and that I am able to carry on because of it and not in spite of it."

Ellen. My dear blessed sister Ellen. How differently we'd found our way. We had each other in those terrible days, but it made no difference because we couldn't share the loneliness we felt. But now, it mattered. Edwin had broken our silence, and it lay shattered, ready for us to pick up its pieces. Who knew what we might find in all that brokenness.

I closed my laptop and checked the clock. It was almost ten-thirty, and class started in thirty minutes. I would slide in a little late, I thought, and no one would mind, especially my students. School was the last thing I was thinking about now, but I'd be okay: I knew how to get through a class—I knew how to get through anything. You keep going, one foot in front of the other. You carry on.

CHAPTER 27

After leaving the Rolduc Abbey near midday, we stop in the village of Aachen, Germany. Crossing the border into enemy country might have felt more significant except that, for days, we've been right on the edge of it. In late 1944, intense combat in the streets of this village resulted in approximately five thousand Allied casualties, but ultimate victory led to the breaking of the Siegfried Line and forward movement to the Rhine River. Our father was injured during the Battle of Aachen. We don't know anything about his injury, except that all his life he struggled with back pain "from the war," sometimes wore a protective girdle under his work clothes, and slept with a mattress-sized piece of plywood under his bed. We also know from his journal entries that he was not transferred out of his unit to be treated. And unlike other soldiers' conditions, he does not label himself as "lightly wounded in action" or "LWA."

Mama told us that when he was offered the opportunity to go to officer's training to become a commissioned lieutenant, he turned down the opportunity, "to be with his men," Mama said proudly. It's the same sergeant who didn't linger on his own wounds, even though they would be with him for the rest of his life.

For an hour or more, we wander the streets of Aachen, grab snacks from vendors, watch children playing in an animated fountain. We see no remains of the battle fought here—no plaques, monuments, tributes, dedications, or ruins—but we aren't here to study war. A street festival is underway, and the city blocks are energized and lively. Leaving Aachen, we anticipate a straight shot to Duisburg and only a couple of hours' drive. Easy peasy.

Duisburg is divided by the Rhine River that meanders through the city in northwest Germany. Months after the Battle of Aachen, Allied troops crossed the Rhine just south of Duisburg in a major offensive operation that allowed armies to move swiftly to Berlin. Duisburg, a major site of chemical, iron, and steel production, was the target of Allied bombing. Today, Duisburg remains an industrial city, a sprawling area with the feel of a large metropolis surrounded by many suburbs. The harbor on the Rhine is one of Germany's largest inland ports, and the influence of the steel industry is visible in its architecture and ambience.

Our destination is the Landschaftspark in Duisburg-Nord, Germany, once a coal and steel production site, now reimagined into a popular park. Within the park is a hostel where we will stay for the night. Gabi, my pen pal for ten years, and her extended family are expecting us for dinner. The hostel is a short walk from Gabi's house, and she says it's not hard to find, but when I type the address into our van's GPS, I get nothing but the endless spinning wheel in response. I try inputting Gabi's street address but turn up nothing.

"I can get us to Duisburg from the map," I whisper to Bill, who is driving, "but I can't find the hostel. Let's just keep going. We'll find directions when we get closer." My paper maps show at least a dozen roads leading to Duisburg, so I can't go wrong there. But over a half a million people live in the Duisburg area; we won't pinpoint an address without more guidance.

Bill turns onto the autobahn and suddenly ours is the slowest car on the road until he floors the accelerator pedal and catches up with the swift flow of traffic. In the back seat, Ellen and David have drifted into naps, and Edwin gazes out the window, watching the German countryside. Despite our increased speed, cars whiz by on both sides.

A glance at Bill's face tells me that he's growing increasingly uncomfortable, first with the speed and, second, I expect, from my uncertainty of where we are going, but he doesn't say anything. It's not unusual for him to clam up when he's tense, but it's not helpful, and the tightening of his lips and the squint of his eyes always give away his worry. I don't say anything but search more frantically for directions. I shift from the paper map to the GPS, trying different addresses, tracing highways with my finger. The closer we get to Duisburg, the more anxious I become and the more lost I feel. I don't have Gabi's phone number, which I wish I'd thought to ask for.

After two hours of driving, Bill pulls into a petrol station/restaurant near the Duisburg city limits. We don't need gas, but everyone's hungry, so the back seaters climb out one by one and head to the restaurant.

"Does anybody care that we're lost?" I call after them. Only Bill looks back. "I need something to eat before I can think about that." It doesn't occur to me that we aren't lost—yet. We just don't know where we are going.

While the other travelers line up to order sandwiches and find seats, I stand in the petrol shop checkout line until I reach the cashier.

"I'm trying to get to Duisburg-Nord, to this address." I hold my map in one hand and the name of the hostel in the other. "Can you help?"

The clerk glances over and then away, as though he's looking for backup. "Yes, I will try." I am grateful for his command of English.

I hand him the address, scribbled on a piece of paper. He looks closely, glances at the customers lined up behind me, then passes the map and my note back to me. "I don't know this place," he says.

Behind me in line, a man waits with a to-go sandwich and a

drink. "Where are you headed?" He's in a white shirt and business slacks. I imagine him as a salesman on calls or a commuter headed home from the office.

He seems willing, so I show him my map and the address. He studies it as he pays for his purchases and then turns.

"Follow me. I'll look it up on my GPS and get the directions for you," he says. I walk behind him to the parking lot, climb in the front passenger seat of his SUV, and watch as he punches in the address, his eyes moving back and forth from paper to machine. Only for a minute do I question his kindness and think that climbing in his car might not be the smartest decision.

I glance to the restaurant, and through the glass, see that my traveling companions are clustered together in a booth by the window, munching on sandwiches. Not one of them is looking my way. My heart is beating fast, not from fear but from frustration at my inability to navigate the systems, stress that we'll never find our way to Gabi's, and irritation with my fellow travelers.

"Nothing is showing. Are you sure this is the correct address?"

I assure him I've given him the best information I have. "Then at least can you tell me how to get to Duisburg-Nord?"

Again, he punches numbers and letters into his machine, reads the results, then takes my paper map. "Follow this highway." His fingers trace a route that splits Duisburg and sends us east. I scribble instructions onto a piece of paper. He seems uncertain or else he's second-guessing himself and his willingness to help me. Whatever, I detect he's ready to leave me behind and get on with his day. At least I have something. I can direct us closer to our bullseye, though I still may be far off the target.

Inside, the others are finishing sandwiches. "Did any of you notice I just got out of a car with a stranger? In Germany?"

"You probably shouldn't have done that," says David.

Edwin smiles. "Did you learn anything?"

I growl in response and then leave them to order my own sandwich to go. No one else seems concerned; I feel as if we are driving into pitch darkness, and we'll never find the light.

Back in the car, Edwin takes the wheel, I navigate, and we head east, as the gentleman has suggested. My brother leans back in the driver's seat, grips his right hand around the steering wheel, and says, "Let's go!" In no time, he's hitting speeds of nearly 180 kilometers, or over a hundred miles per hour. I wonder out loud if he's had experience street racing on country roads outside Asheboro as a teenager. He admits nothing. Ellen leans up from the back seat and snaps a photo of the speedometer. "For proof," she says.

My maps tell me we are driving in the right direction, and for the first time today, it feels as if we have a reliable destination, though once we arrive in Duisburg-Nord, I don't know where to go next. Edwin's hotel reservations are not at the Landschaftspark, but at a nearby hotel, the Residenz Oberhausen.

"Check that address," he says. "At least that would get us somewhere."

It feels like a miracle when his hotel's location appears on the screen with step-by-step directions.

"Let's go for it," Edwin says.

We race along the autobahn for a few more miles and then exit into Duisburg-Nord, winding through city streets crowded with cars, bicycles, and pedestrians. Afternoon traffic is heavy, especially around the industrial areas. At last, when I see the sign above the Hotel Residenz Oberhausen, I raise my arms. "Unbelievable. We made it!" Edwin and I high five; cheers arise from the back seat. Whether they are delighted we are no longer lost or are simply glad to be out of the car, I don't know.

We unload Edwin's bags, check him into the hotel, and then crowd around the front desk. The clerk seems confident she can find the Landschaftspark. She types the address into her phone, pulls up directions, and traces them for us on our city map.

As it turns out, we are not far from the Landschaftspark hostel and after all our detours and entanglements, we're only slightly late to meet Gabi and her family. When we pull into the lot, waiting on the sidewalk to greet us are Gabi, her boyfriend, Didi, his daughter, Jessi, Jessi's partner, Melinda, Gabi's daughter, Steffi, and Helga, a family friend. With them are dogs of all sizes, from ankle high to above the waist. Everyone is waving when they see us drive near, and it's time to celebrate.

My son had not been interested in a pen pal when he was in middle school over ten years ago, but I was, so when he brought home the application from Deutschepost Letternet, I filled it out, describing myself as accurately as possible—forty-five years old, married, one child. I love animals, reading, walking, and traveling. I don't care where in the world my pen pal lives. My only language is English with a few phrases in Spanish in my command since college.

I forgot about the application until, months later, a letter arrived from Germany. "Dear Barbara, I am your pen pal friend," it began.

The letter was a brief introduction. Her name was Gabi. She worked in the post office in Duisburg, had one adult daughter, Steffi, who lived with her, and three dogs. "Excuse my English. I hope you speak German."

Through a series of short letters in rudimentary English, our friendship grew. A German colleague wrote short phrases for me to copy into every letter, phrases like, "Hello," "How are you?" "I am fine," and "Goodbye, friend," but those letters said little more than a beginning German vocabulary book. Soon, Gabi and I learned that we communicated best through photos and gifts. At Christmas, she sent large packages filled with presents—chocolates, stuffed animals, jewelry, a homemade scarf, coffee, stollen, and always toys for my dogs. In turn, I sent packages to Germany—barbecue festival T-shirts, Christmas slippers, Hershey's candy, a towel for her newly designed kitchen, anything uniquely American that I could think of.

Then, in 2012, when I received an opportunity to teach a writing workshop in France, Bill and I decided to go to Europe early and meet Gabi and Steffi.

They picked us up at the Duisburg train station early on a Thursday morning. Shorter than I expected—the top of her head barely reached my shoulder—Gabi had blazing red hair, and she was nervous about her bad English as well as her hosting duties. The thirty-some-year-old Steffi, though, was her opposite. Even though she did not know us, she hugged us hard, and the smile on her face was mischievous and welcoming. Steffi's English was slightly better than her mother's. As for Gabi, we understood little of what she said, and she understood us no better. Steffi did her best to translate, and we all laughed often. Gabi and Steffi were delighted by our visit. We were their American friends, and they were enjoying a bit of popularity in her community because we were there.

We feasted that night in 2012 in the backyard garden beside her boyfriend Didi's fish pond. His urban backyard was narrow and deep, and with a proliferation of plants, flowers, fruit trees, and shrubs, it felt separated from the busyness of the surrounding city life. His wooden table, only a few yards from the fish pond where a few koi swam, was large enough for all of us to gather around. We were joined by Gabi's mother and her boyfriend, and Didi's daughter, Jessi, who served as our translator for the evening. Steffi's friend and neighbor, Nikki, also fluent in English, had joined us midafternoon and stayed until well past dinner.

That night, after stuffing ourselves with barbecue, sauerkraut, beer, and ice cream, we were enjoying a moment of quiet around the table. The sun was setting, and frogs at the pond had begun their evening chorus, singing tunes we both understood.

Jessi broke the moment with a question. "So, what do you think of us and Hitler and all that?" Nineteen and a recent high school graduate, Jessi's black hair fell below her shoulders. She flashed a quick smile, as if she knew she was entering a delicate conversation.

I thought I saw the others glancing at one another as though this was something they'd discussed earlier, and Jessi was the one they designated to ask. Everyone paused, waiting for the answer. It's a subject that had been on my mind too.

Since we had landed in Frankfurt a few days earlier, my first time setting foot in Germany, I had not stopped seeing this as the country that, in the 1940s, attempted to take over the world. As the daughter of an American veteran, World War II is most of what I knew of Germany, and my impressions had been forged by American TV and film. The guards at the airport seemed unnecessarily harsh, their guttural speech clipped with a sharpness that was threatening.

But I didn't say any of that. Instead, I gave the question back to Jessi unanswered. "What do you think?"

Steffi spoke in clear English. "We don't."

We learned in the conversation that followed that they didn't know much about the war, because they had not been taught much in school. Didi's father was a soldier, and Didi had heard of a camp nearby where Jewish people were kept, but they didn't know anything about it, and they'd never visited.

They knew little else.

"It is not who we are," Steffi said.

I hadn't learned about the war in school either, I told them, but it was not because the war wasn't taught. My survey courses in American and world history had made it to World War I and, in some years, to the Great Depression. The little bit I did learn had come from movies and television sitcoms and snatches of Daddy's stories.

We Americans and our German friends talked about the war until well past dark when the bugs and mosquitos came out in full. From the Frankfurt airport to this pond-side patio, I found myself shifting my World War II understanding of this country to a new perspective of a progressive modern-day Germany. Perhaps if given the opportunity, or if I'd paid attention to the opportunity I had, I would have learned about the war as well as postwar progress in Europe. On this night, beside Didi's pond, I learned that the German people, at least this family in Duisburg, were not that different from us.

Months earlier Gabi had insisted we spend the night in her house, and we had accepted, not knowing that staying with Gabi meant we would take her bed and she would sleep on the couch. We couldn't change her mind. The next morning, friends and family returned for a breakfast spread almost as bountiful as our dinner.

Before heading back to the train station, Gabi asked Bill and me if she could take our picture to include in her Book of Guests, an album in which she collects names and photos of everyone who visits.

"Of course," we said and stood together, smiling. More photos followed and then hugs and gifts and promises to return.

We had been welcomed into this group of German friends with whom we learned we had much more in common than we do many Americans. They shared their food, their home, their lives, and we were now a part of them. It felt like family, no matter the different languages or our unique stories.

After we said goodbye at the train station, Gabi, Steffi, and Jessi waited on the platform until our train began its slow acceleration out down the tracks, waving as we passed out of sight. Steffi blew a kiss. They felt like kin, the kind you wish for, the kind you choose.

The two years that have passed since we last saw our German friends feel like but a day when we reconnect in the parking lot of the hostel. Gabi's hair is a softer shade of red. Steffi's arms again open wide and squeeze hard to greet us. Even Murphy, her giant dog, wags his tail as though he remembers us.

"You might find them a little rough around the edges," I said earlier to prepare my siblings. I wasn't sure how they would respond to cigarettes, beer, and cultural differences of food and more. I knew if they got to know them, they'd like them. "They're wide open and fun, so just relax and enjoy."

The backyard patio of Gabi's townhouse, walled in on all four sides by concrete, is not much bigger than my little kitchen. The house itself is narrow and four stories high. For tonight's barbecue, Gabi has arranged chairs around a table covered with a plastic cloth and long enough for all fourteen of us gathered to squeeze in tight. We're joined by Gabi's mother and stepfather, Jessi and her partner, Melinda, and a few friends. Each chair around the table is different—the one I'm sitting in is lined with red vinyl latticing on the seat and back, and the one beside me is wood. I picture Gabi scurrying to the homes of each of her family members and friends here, borrowing enough chairs. Food preparations for this patio meal are elaborate and impressive, with every inch of the table filled with food and drink. Gabi is delighted to tell us she called in sick at work today because her American friends were coming for dinner. That's how special our visit is to her.

Steffi is wearing an "I ♥ NY" T-shirt. As though not to be outdone, Jessi shows off the tattoo on her arm that reads, in English,

"Never a failure. Always a lesson," which is paired with Melinda's "Everything happens for a reason." I ask, "Why English?" and Jessi simply smiles. I'd love to know the story behind the tats, the failure, the lesson, but they don't volunteer it, and I don't ask further. Jessi is now a vibrant blond instead of the brunette she was two years ago, and her whole expression seems livelier and edgier. I wonder if Melinda is one of the reasons. Gabi's face lights up, as always, and she is relaxed with us, no longer nervous as she seemed two years ago. Steffi's deep dimples and genuine smile, along with her strong and welcome embrace, have not changed. Murphy, her dog whose head is level with my waist, pads behind her.

Didi wears a tan "I'd rather be fishing" T-shirt and ball cap. With his grizzly face and jeans, he looks as if he's stepped out of a country song. On our first visit, we learned he has a collection of Johnny Cash music that fills a shelf in his house, a fact I shared with Edwin. Now, Edwin puts his hand on Didi's shoulder. "Johnny Cash?"

Didi's face lights up. "Johnny Cash!" he repeats. He motions for my brother to follow him into the house. In a few minutes, they return, a CD player tucked under Didi's arms blasting "Folsom Prison Blues." Both are singing along in English, though Didi sometimes slips to familiar German. They stand arm in arm until the song plays out, then they bow and laugh as the rest of us clap.

Didi and his friend Willi, who sports a handlebar mustache, fire up the homemade grill. Gabi passes out bottles of König Pilsener beer, made in Duisburg, and hands out bowls and bags of munchie food. Ellen devours the peanut-flavored chips, called Flips. Gabi circles the table often, keeping a fresh König Pilsener in front of each of us. The dogs—little Bennie, mid-sized Max, and even the giant Murphy move softly from lap to lap, looking for attention and crumbs. Soon Didi's steaming hot barbecue—chicken, hot dogs, sausages, schnitzel, and beef—is ready. Plates are passed to the grill, are piled high with meat, and passed back. More cold beer arrives. Sauerkraut made earlier in the day by Willie's wife, Helga, makes its rounds. In between courses and seconds, smoke from Jessi's and Melinda's cigarettes drifts into the night sky.

The beer relaxes me, the stress of our drive earlier today washes away with each swallow. I dig into Didi's chicken and sausages, growing more mellow with each bite. It doesn't matter that, besides us, only Jessi and Melinda and sometimes Steffi speak or understand English, or that our German is limited to "Guten morgen!" Abundant laughter erupts over words misunderstood in both languages. We are all laughing, sometimes at words only half of us understand. Jessi, Melinda, and Steffi do their best to translate, but the words don't matter as much as simply that we are here, around this table, and my German family has embraced my birth family as their own. Ellen, Edwin, and even David, who sometimes struggles to relax, seem to be having fun. The universal languages of food and laughter are noisy and inviting, and we are one around the table.

Midway through dinner, I send a text message to Ellen, who is sitting at the other end of the table beside Gabi: "This is who we were fighting against." I watch as she feels the vibration of her phone, lifts it from her pocket, and reads. Glancing over, she smiles.

After dinner, Gabi goes inside briefly and returns with her Book of Guests open to the first blank page. She shows our picture from two years ago and flips forward to the first blank page.

"You must sign my book," she says to Ellen, David, and Edwin. She snaps their individual photographs, and we all pose for group photos which she will include in her book with names. I position our German friends on the stairs rising up to the kitchen and photograph them all, including the dogs.

"Barbara." The sun has set on the backyard patio when Steffi motions me to join her in the kitchen. "I want to ask you something."

I follow behind her, curious. She leans against the counter in the narrow kitchen. "Why are you doing this, this journey?" I feel she is asking for them all, just as Jessi was designated to ask the question two years ago. "I've been following you on the Internet, and I don't understand. What are you doing?"

I choose my words carefully so that Steffi can understand my English. "Our father was in the war. He fought all the way from the coast of France to the Elbe River here in Germany. We didn't know him well since he died young, so we wanted to follow his journey to see what he saw, feel what he felt."

She smiles. "I get it. That is fantastic. The three of you."

She relays to the others, in German, what I have told her. Their expressions convey that Steffi is in fact answering the question they've pondered together, trying to understand.

"Tomorrow when I come for breakfast," I tell Gabi, "I will bring you his picture."

That evening, Ellen leans an arm against the door frame of her room at the hostel. Didi has driven the four of us back, and Edwin drove the van to his hotel. He'll join us for breakfast in the morning.

"I had a great time. They're fun," she says. The evening has been exactly what we all needed.

The next morning, I present Steffi with a copy of the photograph of my father that I've given our other hosts. She hugs me and shows it to Gabi, who responds by opening her Book of Guests and placing his photo on a new page, my father's own page, as though he too has been a visitor in her house.

After breakfast, as we are saying our goodbyes outside their house, two blond-haired boys, one slightly taller than the other, so similar they could be brothers, bounce a ball back and forth until it strikes the edge of the taller boy's shoe, sending it off course and bouncing through us down the sidewalk. Gabi and the family stand on their porch stoop and wave as we pull away from the curb.

CHAPTER 28

The spring after our New Orleans spring-break trip, I accepted an experimental writing class assignment in a dormitory basement on campus. The room was so damp that on Monday mornings we had to wipe down our desks with rough paper towels from the bathroom before we could begin. Even still, sometimes my sinuses would clog. All semester, some students showed up dressed and ready for the day while many others appeared in pajamas or bathrobes and slippers, rolling out of bed to make their way downstairs. One advantage of this dorm setting was if a student overslept, we could wake them up, and they'd make their way downstairs. Sometimes students brought laundry to the washer in the adjoining room, and they'd leave their seats in the middle of class to shift their wet clothes to the dryer. It was a casual class but a good one, and this was a post-spring break, low-energy day.

My students were huddled in groups and discussing assignments or, most likely, the weekend when my phone, tucked in the pencil pocket of my backpack, rang. I'd banned phones in the classroom, a ban not one of my students took seriously. "That's mine," I said, being as obvious as they often were with theirs. "Who's calling me during class?" When I dug it out, Edwin's face appeared on the screen.

I glanced at my class, most of whom had turned their attention to me and were smiling. "It's my brother." To Edwin, I said, "Can I call you back? I'm in the middle of class. Everybody says hi."

"Tell the class I said hi back. I won't keep you but a sec. I've been thinking today, and I wondered if I ever sent you Daddy's letters."

Now this call made sense. It was March 8. I pictured him the day before, reliving March 7, 1969, as he did every year.

"No, you never sent them," I said. I knew about one letter Edwin received shortly before our father died. I'd heard my brother quote from it many times: "Never, never, ever give up," my father had written, words delivered years earlier to a discouraged nation and now to a college student struggling to make it through a semester.

"I know about one. How many are there?"

He hesitates. "I'll just send them."

I hung up and tucked my phone back in the pocket of my backpack. "Don't ever answer your phone in class," I told my students, smiling.

A full week passed before the brown clasp envelope arrived from Augusta. That afternoon, home from school, I dropped my bookbag on the dining room table and slid my finger beneath the seal as I walked to my desk.

Paper-clipped copies of three letters spilled out, and Edwin had written a note of explanation, which placed each chronologically in the timeline of our father's last days.

These letters, he wrote, will hopefully explain why he'd lived his life the way he had, why it seemed to Ellen and me that he hadn't been as present as we would have liked. I spread the three letters, and his introductions, across the top of my desk and began to read.

I thought I knew his story well. After sitting out the fall semester of 1968, he returned to campus in January 1969, with our parents' full support and high expectations from both them and himself. But by February, when the first letter arrived, he was beginning to sink again.

I imagined him plucking the letter from his campus mailbox when he returned from class, taking it up to his dorm room, flopping on the bed, and tearing away the seal. It was on letterhead from the Lumberton office, where our father had been sent for the last several months to help build new mills.

"I am writing a few lines to boost your morale," Daddy began. He didn't understand Edwin's problem. Edwin simply needed to work hard, and if he wanted to transfer to another college, then he would have to get his grades up, and he'd be able to do that. This man, who had grown up in the Great Depression, who had stayed alive for twelve months during deadly combat, couldn't understand why his son couldn't do better. He had been older than Edwin by two years when he joined the National Guard, and the world was a different place then. Young men matured faster, took on the responsibility of jobs and families at younger ages, unlike postwar children who often postponed adulthood until after college. One of Edwin's objectives during those years was to stay out of the Army and out of Vietnam. Staying in college would help him do that.

"When things get rough, just dig in deeper," Daddy wrote, the entire phrase underlined two times.

There's more. "One day you will be the only man of the house. Mother, Ellen, and Barbara will be depending on you for family decisions instead of me. I want you to be prepared to handle them. A quitter cannot handle them."

I read these words and stopped. It felt like a premonition, as if he was giving Edwin instructions for the rest of his life. Did our father know, or at least fear, that his end was near? "This is the letter that put me on notice that Daddy wanted me to 'be prepared,'" Edwin wrote in his note to me.

No doubt those words lay heavy on the young college student as he sat down to study that night and the days and nights that followed. No doubt guilt and some sense of failure haunted him as his struggle continued.

The second letter in the collection was from Mama Bunting. She began with a chatty overview of her day—a thirteen-inch snow had fallen, preventing her and Daddy Bunting from making a trip to Baltimore as they had planned. "Your mother and Barbara have had a touch of the flu," she wrote.

Midway through the letter, our often harsh grandmother with consistently high standards shifted gears and began an encouraging recollection of her own college years, how her studies came with no breaks, even in summer, and yet how she looked back now and realized these were the best times of her life. When she was a college student, her new husband was a soldier, and for one of her years of study, he was in France, fighting, and soon recovering from wounds in an English hospital.

She goes on: "I'm enclosing a dollar that you may get yourself a 'hot dog' and a 'coke' to help you digest this letter as you read it." Mama Bunting was seventy-two years old when she wrote the letter. I pictured her by the window of the breakfast room where the large wooden radio sat on a table in her corner, her stationery spread across the glass top of the yellow wicker table, as she penned her thoughts to her grandson. Edwin wrote that this letter "was most inspiring to me."

The third letter arrived in his campus mailbox the afternoon of March 4, again from our father, who wrote, "I went to see the dr. with my ulcers again. I might have to have another round of x-rays soon. Will let you know later." The letter was postmarked February 28, one week before the surgery.

But he didn't mention surgery, though he knew by then he was having it. He didn't want Edwin to worry, didn't want any excuse for him to not do his best work.

At six o'clock on the morning of March 6, at the same time Mullie Chandler was waking Ellen and me, Mama called to tell Edwin that he needed to come home because his father was not going to live. He was blindsided. He had no clue that Daddy's health was so precarious.

He stood by his father's bedside at four o'clock the following morning and promised he would finish Clemson. He felt his father squeeze his hand.

"This is the essence of everything," Edwin wrote. "These letters . . . define my motivations in life more than I would have ever realized at the time. I read them frequently and always on March 7."

I'd never seen these letters, and I'd never known, though I'd often wondered, what motivated Edwin, what kept him so distant from his family.

I remembered his promise made to me in our family kitchen the morning after Daddy's death, a promise that he couldn't keep, especially while he was working so hard to fulfill a different one made to a different, more important, person. Conflicting promises, conflicting pulls. Does he take care of his sisters in North Carolina? Or does he become the man his father wanted him? Could he have done both? I imagine the guilt, how difficult it must have been to turn his back on his past in order to build a future he promised his father he could achieve.

I got it. I wished I'd gotten it sooner. I wished he'd shared it sooner. I wondered if our mother, who ached so much for Edwin, even in the years when she fully shut down, knew the full breadth of what he was going through.

Dusk had settled outside the windows of my upstairs office. I heard Bill's car pull into the driveway. In a few minutes, he would come through the door, drop his briefcase in the dining room, and join me. We'd have much to talk about over dinner, as I'd share with him Edwin's latest piece of the puzzle of our early years. He was learning as I was learning, listening carefully, helping me make sense of it all. I reclipped the letters, returned them to the clasp envelope, and held them to my chest. So much to hold was on those pages, so many answers to questions I'd asked for so long. So much I had blamed on myself, on Edwin, on all of us, though not one of us was at fault.

CHAPTER 29

The Bergen-Belsen concentration camp is only a few miles off our route to Magdeburg. We exit the autobahn, zigzag through the villages of Bergen and Belsen and into a patch of woods. A small sign tells us we have arrived.

The stillness silences us before we exit the car. It hangs in the air as we walk quietly to the exhibition in the main building, the Documentation Centre. No camp walls remain here at Bergen-Belsen, no barracks, no crematorium, but there are graves and the land where so many suffered and died.

The stark exhibition building provides a single door for entry. Inside, perpendicular to the length of the building, video screens play interviews with survivors. Old faces, men and women, with rivulets of wrinkles, dark, life-worn skin, gray hair or no hair at all. In voices clear and strong and often with a slight accent, the survivors tell of daily life in the camp, the work of the prisoners, meager food, the constant fear of being deported to Auschwitz where they knew death would be certain. They recount friends and family lost to the camp, unbearable separations, survival, struggle, sickness, even after the war. I stop and listen to the ache in their voices:

"I was only twelve."

"I knew how to cook so they sent me to the kitchen."

"I never saw my family again."

"In the early days, nobody knew what was going to happen. Who would have? Later, though, our fate was determined."

Face after face, eyes that had witnessed the worst of circumstances, the extremes of evil, hard-working people who had been living their lives, raising their families, when everything changed. These lucky ones had survived when eleven million courageous others—Jews, Romas, homosexuals, and prisoners-of-war—did not. Mingled with the voices of the living are words of those who did not live, their stories preserved in letters or artwork or in the memories of others. In glass-enclosed cases beneath the video screens, other stories are told through diaries, photographs, memoirs, articles of clothing, shoes, and other remnants of daily life at the Bergen-Belsen camp. A single shoe or a scrap of fabric is enough to bring back to life a face, a mother, a father, a child.

We separate, needing to experience this place in our own heads and at our own pace. Bill moves through museums slowly, reading words, descriptions, and other information plaques. I am drawn to personal stories and click buttons to set every video in motion. I want to see expressions, read body language, hear the voices— their scratchy throats, their strength and desperation for life. I want to give each piece of clothing the name of its owner. I want to bend down and read words, written in a living hand in a diary or letter.

Constructed in 1940, Bergen-Belsen began as a prisoner-of-war camp for French and Belgium prisoners. A year later, in 1941, renamed Stalag 311, it became one of three Soviet prisoner-of-war camps. By the end of 1942, more than forty-one thousand Soviet prisoners in the three camps, twenty thousand from Bergen-Belsen, had died of starvation, exhaustion, and disease. From 1943 until its liberation by British troops in 1945, Bergen-Belsen became an evacuation site for prisoners from other locations. Over fifty-two thousand people died in there from harsh treatment, starvation, and disease, all results of their imprisonment between 1943–1945. Fourteen thousand more died after liberation by the British.

One of those victims was Anne Frank, who, in her diary, wrote of her family's hiding for two years in an annex in the Amsterdam building where her father worked. In August 1944, the Nazis flushed the family out of the annex and sent them by train to Auschwitz. In October or November of 1944, Anne and her sister Margot were transferred to Bergen-Belsen, where they both died, probably of typhus, a few months later. *The Diary of a Young Girl* captured my heart when I was in school; the lesson of her story becomes real to me in this place of death.

I join Bill at the rear of the exhibition hall, just as Ellen is walking back in.

"David and Edwin are at the graves," she whispers. "Just follow the trail."

We pass through the Anne Frank Platz—a concrete walkway dedicated to her memory—and down a narrow path. Behind the Documentation Centre, mounds of earth, thirteen in all, some as wide and long as a basketball court, rise up from level ground. They are mass graves where thousands of bodies were piled one on top of another and buried quickly. An information board tells us that the camp was burned by British forces in 1945 to prevent the spread of typhus. Tens of thousands of unburied bodies were found at the camp, and many survivors died soon after. At each of the thirteen sites, a plaque gives the approximate number of bodies—men, women, and children, including Anne and Margot Frank—whose remains lie permanently inside this holy ground. The grassy mounds seem to rise and fall unevenly as though gasping for breath.

I stand with Bill, not talking, then reach for his hand, and he holds on. A hundred yards from the mass graves, a small cemetery, built years after the war by families of the victims, rests in a quiet corner of the camp. Headstones, erected years after the war and commemorating the lives of sisters, brothers, fathers, mothers, children, and friends buried, fill the cemetery yard. Ellen joins David there, and Bill and I follow. Edwin walks by himself, for once not prompting conversations with strangers or talking with us. He frames careful photographs, as he's done throughout our trip, and then, perhaps realizing photographs can't tell this story, he closes his camera and leaves it to dangle around his neck.

In this sacred space, the stones, erected by family members, honor people whose lives ended here. Most feature Stars of David, and many include biblical verses in English or Hebrew. We linger in front of Margot's and Anne's shared stone, erected by their father, Otto Frank, their stone prominent because of the names but also because of the stark white lettering against the black stone. We walk from site to site, reading names, birth years, and presumed death dates.

It's Anne's face that lingers in my imagination—that bold hair, those questioning eyes—perhaps because it's so familiar. She was my first introduction to the Holocaust. Like the little girl I was, she loved to write. She wanted to tell her story, and she wanted everyone to read it. Her wish came true, but at too high a price. Margot and Anne were not close as children; Margot was three years older with her own friends and interests. But perhaps they lay bunk to bunk here in Bergen-Belsen, holding hands in the night, perhaps saying their prayers, perhaps knocking on the rails of their wood cots when they finished, as Ellen and I once did, perhaps whispering back and forth.

I glance at Ellen, standing with David on the far sidewalk now, and think of all the years we've had together, our silly childhood games, the hard years with Mama, the times when I was older when I stayed with Ellen when I had no other place to go, our trips as adults to Atlanta and Memphis. So much more. There can be no loss greater than what we see here, what can be found in places like this throughout this continent. Despair. Loneliness. Helplessness. Unbearable sorrow. Silence.

The air is still when we gather outside the Documentation Centre and walk to the parking lot. Smoky clouds hover above our heads.

CHAPTER 30

At the Intercity Hotel in Magdeburg, Germany, a middle-aged man with gentle red hair leans forward, studying the photo I'm holding of my father standing on the banks of the Elbe River. It is the same photo I've carried across Europe, presenting it to tour guides as gifts and to my German friend Gabi as a keepsake. I've studied it daily since the night months ago when I first saw it—its lines so crisp, its blacks and whites as distinct as if it were taken yesterday with a digital camera, my father staring straight ahead at the photographer, straight ahead at me. Even though the photograph is seventy years old, the faces are permanently young and jubilant with war's end, three boys from two different countries who all long to go home.

We've gathered around a table in the dining area of the hotel, empty of diners at midmorning. Across the table, maps, newspaper clippings, and articles printed from the Internet spill out from a red folder. Jürgen Ladebeck takes the photo from my hand and examines it more closely. Then he tilts his head.

"I believe I know where your father was standing." He has a soft voice, gentle, and I listen closely. "The bridge is gone now, but its ramps are still in place, and the hill, of course. We call it Windmill Hill." He points to the mound in the background of the photo, the highway bridge before it, the ramp leading up to the bridge. "It's grown up a bit with shrubs and weeds, but I can find the spot. I'll take you there if you'd like."

My breath catches. He might as well have said, "Your father is alive," for how energized I suddenly feel. I'm ready to go right now to the river.

I don't know how the other travelers feel. We've been in Europe for almost three weeks now with little break in our schedule. Edwin's feeling much better since his rest at the Rolduc Abbey, but now Ellen and David have started coughing, blaming the pollen that is growing thicker the further east we go and the deeper we are into spring. In these short weeks, we've gone from the cold rain of late winter in France to early spring sunshine in Germany, and the temperature changes and seasonal pollen are taking their toll on me as well. So far, only Bill still feels fine.

I glance at Ellen, whose puffy eyes remind me that her allergies were set off by all the cigarette smoke in Duisburg two nights earlier. Bill still hasn't come downstairs to the lobby. Edwin sits with his elbow bent, his chin leaning on his hand, studying Jürgen, this stranger. My brother is tired but he has told me how much this trip has meant to him so far, and he wants to see it through. His regret over not meeting Philippe Krings gnaws at him.

We'll never get this opportunity back, and I don't even ask the others before I say, "If you could do that, we would love it."

Jürgen's mouth turns up in a quick smile. "Yes, I'm happy to."

He is as shy as he is soft-spoken, and his bright eyes tell me he is delighted to be here. He's taken the day off from work for our visit, he told me in an earlier email, and he is eager to show us around. He was our last guide to be arranged—found in a chance Google search—and, in many ways, he is the most crucial, at this ending point of war and the end of our journey.

I slide into the front passenger seat beside Jürgen, who will drive our rented van today as we tour the countryside around Magdeburg. We'll head east to coincide with the route of the 30th Infantry as they raced across Germany in the early spring of 1945. My father's journal describes this "rat race" to Berlin—their instructions to get there as quickly as possible—as "leapfrogging," as the entire army of tanks, trucks, and soldiers stagger their movement for ultimate speed—one group making progress while others take a short rest. After lunch we will trace that hasty advance, Jürgen tells us, driving through captured German towns all the way toward the Elbe.

For all six of us to fit in the van, Bill volunteers to take the back-back seat, a child-size fold-down essentially in the trunk. I glance back at him as Jürgen starts the engine, his face tight with frustration. Of all the travelers, Bill might be the one most likely to listen to Jürgen's stories and take notes on what we see and learn. But in the back-back seat, he'll struggle to hear, and his visibility of the landscape will be obscured. I am grateful for his volunteering, which will allow Edwin and Ellen a closer view. I shrug to show my helplessness and my gratitude; when he sees me, he looks away.

From my shotgun seat, the countryside around Magdeburg looks lush and fertile and as alive with color as any place we've seen in Europe. New wheat fields and miles of yellow wildflowers line the roadsides, and modern windmills, hundreds of them with their spinning propellers, populate the meadows like silver crows.

An hour from Magdeburg, we stop for pizzas and salads in the little town of Königslutter. After Jürgen helps us read the menu and order our selections, he tells his story, which he has shared only briefly with me through our emails.

"My father was drafted as one of Hitler's boy soldiers when he was sixteen late in 1944. In April of 1945, he decided he'd had enough, and he raced across the border of northern Germany and turned himself in to the British. He was home shortly afterward."

He pauses when our server arrives with salads on a tray. After a sip of Coke, he continues.

"My father was fascinated by the war, even though he was a young boy when he was in it. When I was in school, our part of

Germany was under Soviet control, so we were taught the Soviet perspective of the war. I have had to learn the American story on my own. There has been little information available, and it has been difficult at times." Over the years, he has found books, interviews, maps, and data that have filled in gaps for his personal study.

Climbing back into the van after lunch, he tells us, "Not many Americans come through here anymore. In fact, you are the first in a long time." We pass through sleepy towns with few people out on the streets, and the only signs of life are an occasional dog sleeping in a yard or a car passing by. It's a warm spring day, sun magnified by the glass windows of the van. Jürgen's window is down, and I lower mine. The cross breeze feels good. I glance back to see that Edwin's eyes are closed, Ellen and David are fading, and in the back-back seat, Bill has dropped his head. I check to see if Jürgen has noticed, but his face gives no indication. He keeps his eyes on the road ahead.

What's remarkable to me as we move from town to town is Jürgen's knowledge of each locale and the history he recalls. He says, "They captured town after town, each of these villages we are driving through, sometimes several in one day, but it wasn't much of a capture. Nobody resisted. Any troops remaining here had long fled." They were heroes in the eyes of many Germans who were running out of food and supplies, and those who once had faith in their leader had lost it. "Time after time," Jürgen says, "the town officials were so glad to see the Americans that they gave them the key to the city."

I pictured the caravan of jeeps, tanks, trucks, men in formation arriving. Young children must have met them at the edge of town, ushered them in, shouting and celebrating, and perhaps a boy got lucky enough to catch a ride on a US Army truck and maybe take a cigarette from a GI.

North of Wolmirstedt, which Jürgen points out served as headquarters of the 30th, he turns off the highway and stops at the edge of a field. "We'll walk down this road a little way to a clearing. There is a place I believe you'll want to see."

The countryside is sparsely populated, and occasional houses peek out from a row of sycamores along the gravel road we all walk down. Bright blue washes across the sky. The gravel road ends at a field of lush grass, and a steep hill rises before us toward a rolling skyline to the west. Railroad tracks, still in use, are visible at the foot of the hill.

Farlesleben, he tells us. Here, soldiers from the 30th Infantry Division seized a train bound for the Theresienstadt concentration camp. More than two thousand Jewish prisoners from Bergen-Belsen were packed into cars, most likely being transported to their death. It was April 1945. When the doors opened and the prisoners were assured the men with guns were American rescuers, they spilled from the train cars, weak from starvation and disease, but overjoyed at their unexpected liberation. Some crawled to the hillside. Others hugged one another, many cried. Some were too tired or too weak to cry. When the cars were empty of the living, soldiers found many dead bodies on the boxcar floors.

The hill today is just a hill. The tracks look like ordinary railroad tracks, and the freight train that rumbles through as we survey the field might be a freight train headed to Paris carrying goods between the two neighboring countries.

"You might have seen photographs of the liberation," Jürgen says. I have. One in particular: a woman, thin, crying, a scarf tight around her black hair, is running up the hill. One hand grips the hand of a young child, and the other reaches toward the camera, her face breaking into the first smile in perhaps months or even years. Behind her, more children raise their arms. That they are free must seem a miracle.

This grass, these woods. I shiver despite the heat. Days earlier, Jürgen tells us, members of the 30th had liberated Weferlingen, a subcamp of Buchenwald concentration camp. Our father did not participate in either rescue, but chances are, he and his fellow soldiers heard about them as they boarded US Army trucks bound for Berlin. Our father never spoke to us about the Holocaust, but I believe he clung to us more tightly because of it.

"There should be a monument. At least a plaque," Bill says. It seems a small token for the magnitude of this place. Jürgen nods. The tracks, hidden by tall grasses and a hill pass through a tunnel marked by graffiti—the only reminders of that horrific traffic of human beings. White blossoms of pollen drift around us, settling on our shoulders.

"Do you still want to find the place of your father's photograph?" Jürgen asks as we are walking back to the van.

"Yes," I say. "Do you have time?" He's been texting his wife since lunchtime, back and forth. She wants to go shopping late this afternoon for a new range for their kitchen, and already the sun is descending to the western horizon.

"Yes, of course," he says.

"And your wife?"

"She will understand. It is more important that I can do this for you."

We are approaching Magdeburg from the north. We've circled the area and seen the outlying countryside and many villages, tracing the arrival of American soldiers. We pause at the A2 highway bridge that crosses the Elbe River, take the first exit past the bridge, and circle through a patch of woods until we come to a clearing. Jürgen pulls the van to a stop.

"In here," he says, climbing out. He pushes back branches to reveal a small path. When he sees our hesitation, he steps in first, working his way through a brush to an open field with a backdrop of dense trees and the water of the Elbe flowing swiftly beyond. It's a quiet afternoon and, despite traffic on the bridge, the lapping of the waves as they touch the bank is peaceful. The water itself, though, is industrial, murky.

Jürgen stops. "Look beyond those trees—they've grown up a bit—and you can see the ramps coming off the bridge, just as they are in your photo. The bridge itself is no longer there, but the ramps are the same. Now look where the A2 highway still runs east to west." He holds the photo, turns right, as though framing it again. "See the hill in the background? That's Windmill Hill. I am certain this is the exact spot where your father stood."

A thick cluster of trees—oaks, maples, sycamore, and others I recognize—have grown up in this once sparse place, the Elbe River courses through this flatland, and grass of this small patch is uncut. Sixty-nine Aprils ago, this ground was abuzz with activity, hundreds of soldiers speaking different languages, worn out from war but thrilled by the significance of this moment. As my father draped his arms over the shoulders of the two Soviet men, all three smiles wide and true as the Elbe, officers gathered nearby, shaking hands, slapping backs, passing cigars. The war was over.

"Why don't you three get a photo," Jürgen suggests.

Edwin, Ellen, and I come together in the center of the clearing. "Here? Here?" I say, shuffling right, left. I want my feet exactly in his boot tracks, not to the left or right of them. Ellen reaches her hand around my waist, and Edwin's arm drapes my shoulder. With both arms, I bring them together in a hug. There's the slightest lift of breeze, afternoon sun from the west outlines our faces as we stand with our backs to the river. Jürgen snaps the photo.

It feels like holy ground. It feels like home.

But that's not all. With the hum of afternoon traffic in the background, the water of the Elbe still murmuring, and sun so strong on my shoulders, I feel the hug of a green plaid shirt, warm and alive.

If I listen, I will hear his voice.

Epilogue

A thin current runs between what we see and what we don't see, between what is and what isn't, and truth flows somewhere between the banks, rippling in and out, splashing over rocks, and carrying us along like leaves adrift.

Memory is like that, shaping a past that might or might not have been, eroding centuries-old rock formations, sculpting change, smoothing surfaces.

In the summer of 1957, my mother and father, Edwin, Ellen, and I loaded up the Chevy and headed to White Lake, North Carolina, three hours from home. I was three years old, already boasting a thick crop of brown hair in a pixie cut that my mother pinned away from my face with colorful barrettes and rubber bands. Ellen, at five and a half, was my blond partner, and though I was still baby-fat chubby, I was catching up with her in height. Edwin, age eight, his hair close-cropped for summer, was rail thin, his skinny legs as wiry as a chicken's. Already, he wore the mischievous grin he'd have all his life—everything fine, everything fun, every day a good day, at least on the outside.

Our mother was at her stylish best that summer. Thirty-two, sleek and strong in a black bathing suit, her dark, wavy hair in a close-cut bob popular in the fifties. Daddy, too, still a young man, was comfortable in the uniform of lake life—bathing suit, bare chest and belly, and no shoes. He loped a little when he walked, almost as if he had a limp or a slightly misaligned leg. If it's true that children learn to walk by mimicking their parents, then I got my own lope from him, and my son has it too. What we pass down without even realizing we do.

Years later, my mother talked about White Lake with a dreaminess in her voice. She loved being near water, loved the sun. Every summer after this one, we headed for the beach, and every year after Daddy died, no exceptions, we found ourselves by the ocean. But this one time, this one summer, we went to White Lake.

Thing is, not one of us children, not even Edwin, the oldest, remembers a single detail about this White Lake trip—why we went, who we went with, how long or where we stayed. It was a one-season adventure; why we never returned, we'll never know.

But two photographs document our time there, a sequence that tells a story as surely as the water in the lake still splashes against the banks. In the backdrop of the first image is the idyllic setting of White Lake—luscious live oaks draping the water, slatted wooden homes along the banks, each with its own private dock, rowboats and sailboats tied to those docks and bouncing with the waves, groups of children swimming in the shallows, a few men heading out in the morning to fish.

I imagine that morning, perhaps standing on the shoreline, my father saw the little rowboat, perhaps belonging to a friend, and said, "Let's take the children for a ride. They'd love it."

My mother hesitated, as she always did, for fear we might fall out, or one of us could get hurt, but he was the playful one, which is what she always loved about him, and she agreed. We waded out, ankle deep, our parents steadied the boat while we climbed in, his camera dangling around his neck and knocking against the boat's side. Then he backed away, while she held on.

Three children in a miniature rowboat. Even though it's a black-and-white photo, I imagine the boat red, because it would have been red. There were no oars and not even room for oars in the tiny boat. Ellen and I sit side by side in the middle seat, she in her plaid bathing suit that bubbles out below the waist to the top of her thighs, and I'm in a similar, flowered suit, though more blousy, something a baby would wear. Edwin sits behind us on the rear bench of the boat, so tall by then that his head rises above our heads, that wide grin across his face. Mama stands in the water, leaning forward, holding the edge of the boat as if to steady it, and her eyes are watching us children. Mother hen, we used to call her, always protecting her chicks. The water rises only to her mid-calf, so even if we capsized, we wouldn't be in danger.

There's a fifth person in this photograph, not visible on the paper itself, but so present that the picture isn't complete without him. Our father, the cameraman, always taking the pictures so he's rarely in them, is squarely in the middle of this one in that we three children are looking right at him, smiling like he's just said something funny. He probably has. There would be no photograph if not for him. There would be no smiles from the children in the boat. There would be no children.

Then he turned to Mama and urged her to lift her hand away and let us float. Again, she must have hesitated, unsure. All she ever wanted was to keep us safe, to keep us from getting hurt.

Reluctantly, she dropped her grip from the back of the boat, and she stepped away, just barely out of camera view. Just then, a wave or a wake from a passing boat caught ours and carried us further out, far enough that no parents were nearby, and he snapped the second picture.

In this photo, there is no backdrop of houses or docks, not even sky, just water in all directions, encompassing the boat. Three children, alone in a tiny rowboat. No matter that they are so close to shore and the water is so shallow. No matter, too, that the parents—overprotective mother and playful father—are within arms' length.

In the photo, it is just us three. Again Edwin and Ellen look away. I'm holding my temples, a kind of Edvard Munch moment of fear, or maybe just to swat a gnat that's swarming my face.

That's it. Three children in a boat and vague memories of Mama's story of the summer we went to White Lake, all we have as proof the trip ever happened.

That and memory of his voice, off camera—that soothing, confident voice I haven't heard in so long I have forgotten the tenor of it, but so clear I can hear it through the years, over the rippling waters.

"It's all right, Tina. Let them go. They're going to be fine."

acknowledgments

I couldn't have asked for better siblings than Edwin and Ellen, who have been my North Stars since that day when I said, "Okay, let's do this together." They've questioned my memory and explored their own; they've read drafts, corrected facts, and added new perspectives to my recollections. We've shared tears and bear hugs and sloppy "I love you" moments that would embarrass most people, especially our children. I wouldn't have a story without Edwin and Ellen; I wouldn't have the rich, rooted feeling I get being around them; I wouldn't laugh so hard, share so much, or see so much of myself in them. They are cowriters of this story, cocreators of my life, and I am eternally grateful that they are back in it.

We were joined on our adventure by spouses, David and Bill, both lovers of history with knowledge of the war that helped me see not just our little piece of it but also the larger picture and how our story fit in. Each spouse offered insightful responses to early drafts. Edwin's wife, Deb, didn't travel with us, but her sense of adventure, exploration, and fun helped shape our excursions and continue to shape our growing family.

When our ideas for this trip began to take shape, we thought we were doing something that no one had ever attempted; we quickly learned that 30th Infantry Division historians, enthusiasts, veterans, families of veterans, and young soldiers serving today are everywhere, and this trip and this book would not have been possible without them. Frank Towers, who served right beside my father, was an endless source of facts, detail, history, and firsthand experience. Every one of our guides in Europe, as soon as they heard what we were doing, stepped up with enthusiasm and expertise, taking days off work and away from families, feeding us, treating us like we were the heroes. Each taught us something about gratitude, freedom, injustice, and the importance of history and family. Our friendships have continued to grow, united by an eighty-year-old war and a connection that bridges distance, language, and history. To this day, the phrase that still stops me is, "Your father would have been right here," a phrase repeated by each of our guides. They knew what we wanted; they understood that we cared less about the facts of war and more about one man's journey through it.

Noël Sarrazin and his furry companion, Heidi, along with Charles Lebrun, Sonia Leprevost, Mayor Hervé Desserouer, and Deputy Mayor Jean-Paul Briend welcomed us to Mortain, France, with fanfare given to returning soldiers. Vince Heggen and Marcel Verwilghen in Belgium understood the importance of each young soldier, especially those buried in some of the most beautiful cemeteries in the world. Hub Schetters and Catharina Scholtens in Kerkrade shared the intensity of war, and Philippe Krings helped us understand personal and family sacrifice. Jürgen Ladebeck knew instinctively how we needed to end our journey, and he made it happen. Sadly, three of our friends—Frank Towers, Charles Lebrun, and Philippe Krings—have left us since the trip, but they leave behind their rich experiences, not forgotten, which they have generously shared with the world. I am grateful that our lives touched while we were still able to hear their stories in their own words, to see fresh tears spill down their faces so many years after the war.

I am also incredibly grateful for a different perspective offered by our modern-day German friends, Gabi, Didi, Steffi, Jessi, and all their friends and family in Duisburg; our bonds formed from curiosity and hospitality and solidified by barbecue, beer, Johnny Cash, big dogs, and a lot of laughs and hearty hugs.

Acknowledgments

My travel research was supported by a Regional Artist grant from the Arts Council of Winston-Salem and Forsyth County, funded by the NC Arts Council and Duke Energy. I am also indebted to the University of North Carolina at Charlotte for their travel funds and considerable personal support.

This book began as short essays that were charted, drafted, shifted, shaped, shuffled, revised, and polished in a wide variety of settings, most of them surrounded by trees, a variety of wild critters, and sometimes considerable rain. Willapa Bay AiR nourished me in all ways physical and creative; Wildacres, my home away from home, always reminds me I'm on solid ground; the Studium at Saint Benedict's Monastery in St. Joseph, Minnesota, and the sisters' a Capello blessing, sung on my parting morning, will stay with me forever; the Hambidge Center for the Arts and the Hermitages at Valle Crucis gave me solitude at the top of steep hills. All are places that put their stamp on this story in unique and creative ways.

Early essays appear in the anthology, *Reflections on the New River* (McFarland, 2015); and in journals, *Cumberland Review, Kestrel, South Writ Large*, and *r.kv.r.y. The Dispatch* in Lexington, North Carolina, followed our journey. Media outlets in Augusta, Georgia; Greensboro, North Carolina; and Asheboro, North Carolina, have told excerpts of our story. I am grateful for each publication's enthusiastic support of the project. It was my friend Pat Boswell who said what I knew immediately to be true: "You need to write those essays as one memoir." It wasn't as easy as I hoped it would be, "just to seam around the edges." In essence, I started over, but I knew Pat was right, and her words drove me.

How do I thank a global pandemic? How do I thank a well-timed retirement? Both gave me the freedom I needed to paint my house and write a book. Beth Terrell (a.k.a. Jaden Terrell), hard-boiled crime writer with the best intuition for structure I've ever seen, helped me make a plan. I'm still using those index cards. My

Acknowledgments

A Room of Her Own (AROHO) friends formed a virtual circle around me exactly when I needed them. Penelope Gay Dane and Carol Fox Prescott remain inspirations and reminders to dance and to breathe! Darlene Chandler Bassett, several time zones away, rescued me from the woods more than once.

My early readers, beta and curious, gave the book close readings. I was humbled by the attention each reader paid to the words, by the depth and detail of their comments, and by their enthusiasm and support. Thank you to this remarkable group of brilliant writers and first readers: Cindy Brookshire, Lynn Raymond, Penelope Gay Dane, Verda Jaroszewski, and Meg Morgan.

Behind all my words are the voices of my long-time poetry group—Diana Pinckney, Dede Wilson, Gail Peck, Barbara Conrad, and Rebecca McClanahan. In addition to many jewels of writing wisdom, they taught me to stick with a piece until it's the best it can be. My new writing group has astonished me with patience as I've worked for as long as they've known me on this project. They've critiqued multiple drafts of multiple scenes, and over the years must have read the entire book many times. I am grateful for the friendship and support and patience of Lisa Underwood, Tere Wagner, Kate Carey, Christy Hamrick, Naomi Faw, and Pat Boswell.

I will be forever indebted to my lifelong teacher and friend, the late Fred Chappell, who taught me that being a writer is not about ego or fame or legacy but persistence, generosity, and love.

Tracy Crow, literary agent with a big heart, entered my life at a time when I needed someone who believed in the project. Tracy believed from the beginning, and before I knew it, I was in conversation with Michael McGandy, director of the University of South Carolina (USC) Press, who saw a story in this rough manuscript that he thought was worth telling. Tracy is always at the receiving end of my texts and emails, encouraging, suggesting, commiserating, advising. What a gift Tracy has been in so many ways! Working with Michael has elevated my appreciation for clarity and poetry. I have never had an editor who read my work with the precision, toughness, and insight that he has given this project, and I am deeply indebted to his belief in this book since its raw beginnings.

Others on the USC Press team have been wonderful collaborators: Kerri Tolan, production editor; Ashley Mathias, digital publishing coordinator; Dianne Wade, marketing assistant; Cathy Esposito, marketing director; and Kim Doran, copyeditor. To everyone on the USC Press team who has provided ideas, development, and so much more, I am very grateful.

My Lexington community has supported my writing for as long as I've been planted here, and I am surrounded by so many friends and neighbors who keep me going. My UNC-Charlotte community for so many years was my home at the other end of my commute. It's cliché to say, but it's true that my students through the years have taught me more about writing and life than I've taught them. I remember you.

Finally, it's those I share my life with who have loved me, given me time and a place to write, let me go off on retreats and residencies and welcomed me home when my time away was over. Bill, with whom I share so much, including a love of words and years of dinner table discussions that sometimes go well into the night; Will, the best son anyone could ever hope for; Mary Ellen, the woman with whom he chose to share his life who has become an essential part of my own; the new members of my extended family—Neil, Ann, Meredyth, and Seb; and my boys, Ward and Tripp. No words have been invented that can adequately express the joy you've brought to my life. My crazy, sweet Colby—I wonder who rescued whom?

This book releases something for me. It's a story I've lived with, struggled through, run from, embraced. Finally, it's a story I own, the one that has made me who I am, good and bad. To all who have met me somewhere along the path: you have changed my life, and I am grateful. I hope that I have given back even a small portion of what I have received.